# estherpress

## Books for Courageous Women

### ESTHER PRESS VISION

*Publishing diverse voices that encourage and equip women to walk courageously in the light of God's truth for such a time as this.*

### BIBLICAL STATEMENT OF PURPOSE

*"For if you keep silent at this time, relief and deliverance will rise for the Jews from another place, but you and your father's house will perish. And who knows whether you have not come to the kingdom for such a time as this?"*

Esther 4:14 (ESV)

What people are saying about …

# YOU ARE UNSHAKEN

"If you've ever wondered if there is purpose for your life or if you are valued, Laura Krokos has written a book just for you. Her conversational style, her creative analogies, and her practical applications will assure you that *you are unshaken* and God has beautiful purposes for you. You will discover the irrefutable evidence that God is in control of the magnificence of creation and of the tiniest detail of your life."

**Judy Douglass,** writer, speaker, director for Cru Women's Resources, author of *When You Love a Prodigal* book and podcast

"Infused with Scripture and powerful stories, *You are Unshaken* is a book that will help you understand two foundational truths: the nature of God and the identity of a Christian. In a world filled with constant attacks on both, Laura points us to biblical truths that help shape our thoughts and emotions in a Christ-centered, life-changing way."

**Katie Orr,** author of *Secrets of the Happy Soul* and the FOCUSed15 Bible study series

"In *You Are Unshaken*, Laura reminds us that we become what we gaze at. And if we are gazing at a god made in our own image … or a culture falling apart around us … or a world plighted with darkness … is it any wonder we find ourselves anxious, distraught, and anemic? Yet the solution is simple: fix our eyes on our great God. Drawing on decades of ministry,

Laura shares seven core truths we can all "gaze" upon to shape us into women who walk with unshakable confidence. Well done and much needed in our day."

**Arabah Joy,** author of *Trust without Borders*, blogger, and Bible study teacher at Sojo Academy

"Truly, Laura has written the book we need for such a time as this. When the world feels dark and chaotic, we must be able to recognize the Enemy's lies and combat them with the truth of God's Word so we can stand firm. In *You Are Unshaken*, Laura blends biblical perspective perfectly with her own personal experiences, and I especially appreciate the Scripture and 'truth charts' for reflection at the end of each chapter. This is a book I will read more than once."

**Amy L. Hale,** writer, speaker, Bible teacher

"I have always appreciated Laura's relentless passion for ministry. In her new book, *You Are Unshaken*, she pours her heart onto the page. With an easy-to-use format, heartfelt stories, and useful applications, she guides the reader toward biblical transformation. This book will be an amazing resource not only for you but also for the women in your family, in your church, and on your street."

**Stacey Thacker,** author of *Threadbare Prayer*

# YOU ARE
# UNSHAKEN

LAURA KROKOS

AN INTERACTIVE
BOOK

With 7-Session
Video Series

# YOU ARE UNSHAKEN

## FINDING SECURITY IN GOD IN AN UNCERTAIN WORLD

estherpress

Books for Courageous Women
from David C Cook

YOU ARE UNSHAKEN
Published by David C Cook
4050 Lee Vance Drive
Colorado Springs, CO 80918 U.S.A.

Integrity Music Limited, a Division of David C Cook
Brighton, East Sussex BN1 2RE, England

Esther Press, David C Cook, and related logos are trademarks of David C Cook.

The website addresses recommended throughout this book are offered as a resource to you. These websites are not intended in any way to be or imply an endorsement on the part of David C Cook, nor do we vouch for their content.

Details in some stories have been changed to protect the identities of the persons involved.

ISBN 978-0-8307-8472-1
eISBN 978-0-8307-8473-8

The Team: Susan McPherson, Stephanie Bennett, Jeff Gerke, Judy Gillispie,
Elise Boutell, James Hershberger, Susan Murdock
Cover Design: James Hershberger
Cover and Interior Artwork: Laura Krokos

Printed in the United States of America
First Edition 2023

1 2 3 4 5 6 7 8 9 10

110222

*To Asher, Uriah, Eden, Malachi, Willow, and Asa. I pray you live life unshaken as you keep your eyes on the author and perfecter of your faith and take big steps of faith to make Him known.*

# CONTENTS

# Acknowledgments

This book has been the work of many hands and the result of many prayers. I am especially thankful to my husband, who was willing to wrangle our six kids to allow me time to write. I'm also incredibly thankful for the gift and pleasure it has been to work with Jeff Gerke and learn from his expertise, Susan McPherson in her pioneering spirit of making Jesus known, Judy Gillispie and her wisdom with words, and the rest of the David C Cook team. Thank you so much for sharing your enthusiasm, expertise, and confidence. Thank you to my wonderful agent, Keely Boeving of WordServe Literary Group.

I'm also very grateful for my pastor, Colby Corsaut, who was willing to give this manuscript a theological read-through in order to have another set of eyes make sure everything it says matches God's Word, and for the Missional Women prayer team.

My loving parents, Sandy Peterson and Steve Heany, have been a continual source of encouragement and have deeply influenced me and given me confidence and perseverance to move forward in the things the Lord has for me to walk in. Thank you for your example of love and support.

And lastly, I'm so honored to get to share many of my friends' stories. I can't believe I get to know and have the honor of being friends with such brave, godly women. Thank you, Abigail and Amy. I'm so honored the Lord joined this team together, and my heartfelt desire is that He would be loved and trusted more as a result. I pray that the Lord would use this book to help people see Him more truly and trust Him more fully.

# Introduction

When I was in college, I went on a mission trip to Nepal. Steve, Joel, and I shared the gospel with a guy named Ram. He gave his life to Christ and was so excited about the gospel that he wanted his family to hear it. So he invited us to his village to tell them about Jesus.

What we didn't realize at first was that his village was not exactly nearby. So we began the exciting and terrifying twenty-four-hour journey to get there. We started on a bus bursting with people, luggage, and chickens. During the ride, a strange Nepali lady, whom I didn't know from Adam, rested her head on my lap as if it were totally normal.

We continued through the extremely windy mountain pass, overlooking a huge drop-off on one side of the road, going what seemed to me seventy miles per hour … until we came to a halt for quite some time. Turns out the road had washed away and they had to rebuild it "real quick." We would then be the guinea-pig bus to test the newly built road. We made it through without being washed down the cliff and finally arrived at the last stop. This was when our uphill trek—what felt like a twenty-two-mile climb—began. I probably should remind you that Nepal is home to the tallest mountain in the world, Mount Everest. The Himalayas are no joke.

I'd thought I was somewhat in shape. Ha! It felt like walking upstairs wearing a backpack as big as me. I could take only a few steps without having to stop for breath. Ram, along with most Nepali people, was very short. I'm five foot four. Not exactly a giant. But I sure felt like one standing by Ram. Well, since I was holding up our group, Ram took my backpack from me and our pace picked up.

Next, we came to a wooden bridge you would expect to see in an *Indiana Jones* movie. Rickety. Swinging. A hundred and fifty feet in the air. Crocodiles at the bottom. (Well, this was over twenty years ago, so maybe the bridge wasn't so bad. But it's my story, okay?) Against my better judgment but thinking of the eternal souls of Ram's family, I crossed that thing.

Just as I stepped off onto terra firma again, I looked back at the bridge and saw, to my horror, multiple men the size of Ram carrying couches and fridges on their backs. Couch*es*—plural! Two of them fit inside each other. And another guy with a fridge! I was seriously in shock. I couldn't even carry my backpack, and these guys—smaller than me, I might remind you—were carrying heavy furniture up what had to be a twelve-thousand-foot mountain! Need I say their muscles looked like they were going to bust out of their skin?

At one point during this trek, we talked about praying. Ram had no idea what prayer was, so we told him he should just talk to God. So he did. He began to describe to God where we were, what we were doing, what the day was like, and so on. "It's a pretty cloudy day, and I'm taking my new friends to my village," and on and on in what I thought was the cutest childlike prayer. But then I realized Ram had no idea that God knew everything. What a huge understanding of God that I totally took for granted.

## Who Is God, Really?

The truth is that many people in other countries have no understanding of God at all. And though in the United States we are greatly blessed with a lot of knowledge about

God, we can sometimes act just like Ram, believing that God knows nothing of our situations or is powerless to do anything about them. And what a big deal that is!

A. W. Tozer famously said, "What comes into our minds when we think about God is the most important thing about us.… And the most portentous fact about any man is not what he at a given time may say or do, but what he in his deep heart conceives God to be like."[1]

Bill Bright, the founder of Campus Crusade for Christ (now Cru), said something similar: "How you view God and His involvement in your life touches every facet of who you are. Everything about your life—your desires, motives, attitudes, words and actions—is influenced by your perception of God."[2]

Did you catch that? Both of these godly men are making the same point: that what we believe about God is the most important thing about us and that it affects every part of who we are.

Thankfully, we have a God who loves to reveal Himself and who goes out of His way to motivate us to seek Him. In Exodus 33:18, God orchestrates things in such a way that moves Moses to cry out to God, "Please, show me Your glory!" (AMP). Moses is basically saying, in the words of Max Lucado, "Flex your biceps. Let me see the *S* on your chest. Your preeminence. Your heart-stopping, ground-shaking extraspectacularness.… *Would you stun me with your strength? Numb me with your wisdom? Steal my breath with a brush of yours?*"[3]

And our great God answers with a "Yes!" "I will cause all my goodness to pass in front of you" (Ex. 33:19), and He gives Moses a glimpse of who He is: "The LORD passed before him and proclaimed, 'The LORD, the LORD, a God merciful and gracious, slow to anger, and abounding in steadfast love and faithfulness, keeping steadfast love for thousands, forgiving iniquity and transgression and sin'" (34:6–7 ESV). God delights in revealing His character to His people. And how incredible is it that we are most deeply satisfied when our beliefs about God are accurate!

Moses wanted to see God's *glory*. What is that? Sparks with angels singing? No, God's glory is the revelation of His nature and character, His attributes. When the Lord

Any time we know something true about God, it's because God revealed Himself to us.

chooses to show us His glory, He opens our eyes to what He is like, revealing how He wants to be known by us.

When Jesus asked Peter, "Who do you say I am?" Peter declared, "The Son of the living God" (Matt. 16:15–16). Jesus then pointed out that it was *God* who had revealed that to him (see v. 17). Any time we know something true about God, it's because God revealed Himself to us.

Pause. Did you catch that? We just aren't smart enough to figure out the timeless God on our own. Any truth you know about God, you know because God opened your mind and enabled you to understand it. He unveiled His character that we may behold Him.

And Paul said that beholding God's glory transforms the beholder: "We all, with unveiled faces, are looking as in a mirror at the glory of the Lord and are being transformed into the same image from glory to glory; this is from the Lord who is the Spirit" (2 Cor. 3:18 HCSB).

As we behold God and begin to understand His vast and magnificent power, our lives cannot help but be transformed. Everything about us will change—our attitudes, actions, motives, desires. For when it comes to spiritual things, we become what we gaze at.

Everything about us is impacted when we see God as He truly is. Therefore, we need to repeatedly remind ourselves and choose to believe what is true about God regardless of our feelings or circumstances. We need to take every thought captive and make it obedient to the Lord (see 2 Cor. 10:5).

We can think of our thoughts and emotions as temperature gauges indicating what we believe about God. And God is the One who reveals Himself, so when we realize we are believing something not true, we need to admit we need Him to help us see and believe Him. We need the Holy Spirit to help us understand when God reveals Himself to us, and that takes humbling ourselves. We need to come to the Lord admitting we can't understand if He doesn't enable us.

We need to repeatedly ...
choose to believe what is true
about God regardless of our
feelings or circumstances.

# How This Study Works

The chapters of this book focus on common lies the Enemy uses. Each lie is a weapon he desires to use to take you out. Chapter by chapter, *You Are Unshaken* exposes the truth of who God is and who you are. At the end of each chapter, there will be an opportunity to go to the Lord with your thoughts and feelings so you can bring them to the surface and expose what you really believe about God. This will enable you to use your sword of the Spirit, which is the Word of God (see Eph. 6:17), and take those thoughts captive and make them obedient to Christ. Remembering God's truth, sovereignty, goodness, and other attributes takes practice and doesn't naturally fall out of us. It takes intentionality.

*You Are Unshaken* is an eight-week Bible study. Ideally, you'll be doing this study with a group (in person or online), because you'll really benefit from sharing your answers with others in the discussion time. But if you're doing this study by yourself, the same structure to the sessions will apply.

I've made seven session videos plus an introductory one to go with this study. You'll watch the introduction video with your group. Then the other seven videos are designed to be watched after reading each corresponding chapter. So, for example, each woman in your group will read chapter 1 independently, and then you'll all get together to watch the chapter 1 video and discuss it.

You can structure your group's meeting time however you'd like, but here's a sample flow to get your thinking started:

---

### *Sample Meeting Flow*
- Snacks and fellowship as you gather
- Greeting and introduction
- Opening prayer
- Recap discussion of the previous week's chapter
- Video watching
- Group discussion
- Prayer requests
- Closing prayer

---

I've placed some helpful resources at the end of this book, which include Scripture lists to affirm your journey to being *unshaken*.

The Enemy wants to distract, discourage, destroy, and lead you into despair. He throws fiery lie-darts at you, seven of which are covered in this book. Each one is combatted by the truth of who God is to help you live an unshaken life.

My hope as I offer this book is that you will live with your head held high in confidence that though you may be struck down, you won't be destroyed (see 2 Cor. 4:9).

*Be sure to watch the introduction video before starting!*

**Access the Videos Here**
https://davidccook.org/prd/unshaken
Access code: Unshaken
Or scan this QR code:

You can find additional
resources to help
your small group at
MissionalWomen.com.

Chapter 1

# You Are Not Hidden

Have you ever been overlooked, underappreciated, or disregarded? Or perhaps someone else received what you hoped for. Have you felt squelched, shut down, overshadowed, or suppressed? Or maybe someone assumed your motives were bad when they weren't. This world is not short on opportunities to be stifled, misunderstood, and trampled on.

From a young age, we hear the Enemy whispering that nobody sees and nobody cares. And why? Because he knows that all human beings, created in the image of God, have an innate desire to be seen, respected, and valued. So he hits us where it really hurts.

But whenever we realize we are believing a lie, we need to intentionally tell ourselves the truth: the truth about ourselves, the truth about God, and the truth about others.

And the truth is that *we are seen*. Every aspect of our hearts—our hopes, dreams, longings, thoughts, and motives—is deeply known.

You are not hidden. You are fully seen, fully heard, and fully known. As we learn more about the God who sees, I hope this truth settles deeply in your soul.

# God Sees You

"Look at me! Look at me!" It's the cry of kids wanting someone to see what they're doing. And not just kids, but the girl who wants the cute boy to notice her and the wife or mom who wants her contribution to be noted. We have a built-in desire to be seen, and that often comes with a negative connotation. But it doesn't have to.

Have you ever thought about why we have a desire to be seen? Because we are the *Imago Dei*. We are made in the image of God, the God who wants to be seen. Ezekiel is pretty straightforward about this. He uses the phrase "they will know that I am the LORD" thirty-four times. God does what He does to reveal Himself, to be seen.

In 2011, I led a mission trip of young ladies to the heart of Cambodia to work with Agape International Missions (AIM), a humanitarian aid and church-planting organization focused on ending the evil of child sex slavery in the country. Cambodia may be one of the darkest places on earth. Child slavery abounds there, and many of the foreign men in the country are there to buy sex. Yet even in this pitch-black, hidden place, God's brightness shines. It was in Cambodia where I reveled more in God as the rescuer and redeemer of the hidden than I had ever thought possible. Even there, I saw God rescuing, teaching, and saving.

At one point, the other leader and I were waiting for the hotel elevator to take us to the lobby, where we would meet our team of fifteen American girls to go to the Khmer Rouge holocaust museum. As we waited, a large white man in his fifties opened his room door, came to sit on the couch by the elevator, and lit up a cigarette. He left his door open, and we saw an underage Cambodian girl dressed in only a man's shirt standing just inside.

Being untrained in how to handle trafficking situations, we motioned to the girl to come to us, and I engaged the man by asking what he was doing with an underage girl. I took his picture, and the other leader went to get hotel security. When I told the man I was going to post his picture all over the internet, he defended his actions by saying, "She liked it." I was horrified.

When security arrived, they asked the girl for her paperwork (which, I guess, was her birth certificate). They let us look at it, and all we could tell was that the entire document was in the local language, except her birth year, which had been whited out and replaced with a year that implied she was twentysomething. Clearly, this girl was trapped in an illegal situation, yet nothing could be done.

When we finally got on the bus, I couldn't hold back my emotions any longer, and I bawled my heart out.

Although this young girl was kept hidden in the most horrific way, she was not unseen by God. Though this young girl was concealed from most people, she was never hidden from the Lord. He knew exactly where she was. Even in her darkest moments, He was fully present. God saw her, heard her, and knew her, even if she didn't realize it at the time.

And just as this young girl wasn't truly hidden, neither are you. No matter what you're up against, you're not hidden. God sees you.

Do you remember the story of Joseph in Genesis? (See chapters 37; 39.) Like the young Cambodian girl, Joseph was sold into slavery. He grew up in a small ranching town in the Middle East, and he was his dad's favorite. He had ten older brothers whose jealousy of him turned to hatred. When his brothers saw opportunity to gain from his pain, they sold him to human traffickers and convinced their dad he had been killed by a wild animal. The traffickers took Joseph to Egypt and sold him to Potiphar, the head of Pharaoh's guards.

Slavery was Joseph's new life. But, loving the Lord, he served to the best of his ability, as though he were serving God. Eventually, he won favor with Potiphar and was put in charge of everything he owned. As Joseph grew older, Potiphar's wife took notice of him. She tried to seduce him, but he wanted to please the Lord above all else, so he ran from her. The wife lied about him to Potiphar, and he was put in jail.

Joseph went from being hidden as a slave to being hidden in a jail cell. But though he was concealed from others, he wasn't hidden from God. God saw this before it even happened.

Amazingly, Joseph's story foreshadows Jesus' story. His life shows us parts of God's heart and character that had not been revealed in Scripture up to that point. His life illustrates what the Messiah would one day go through.

Like Jesus, Joseph was an obedient son. He was stripped of his clothes, which were covered in blood, and was sold for a few pieces of silver. He was a seed of Abraham, and his name would be made great. He would be exalted to the right hand of power. His own people wanted to kill him, and they turned him over to the Gentiles. Through his separation there would be reconciliation for others, and this would bless all families on earth.[1]

Like Jesus, Joseph was falsely accused and punished. He was sent by God to preserve life and was most loved by his father. His brothers didn't believe him or the prophecies that said he would rule. He was given a Gentile bride, and he was used by God to rescue his people from tribulation. His own brothers didn't recognize him, but his identity finally became clear. He was hidden but was eventually seen.[2]

Jesus suffered all these things as well—so He relates deeply to our experiences of being misunderstood, betrayed, hidden, and overlooked.

Maybe you haven't been sold into slavery like Cambodian girls or Joseph, but chances are good you've felt unseen. Maybe you've been overlooked, or maybe your motives were thought to be something they weren't. Maybe someone assumed the worst of you or didn't see what you could bring to the table. Maybe your talents, gifts, motives, perseverance, kindness, or hard work went unnoticed.

Or maybe you're the one doing the hiding. Sometimes, whether because you feel shame over what's been done to you or guilt for what you yourself have done, you might decide it's just more comfortable to hide than to be seen, heard, and known.

Ultimately, however, hiding only contributes to our feelings of insecurity and shame. Hiding gives only a facade of security that in the end fails and robs us of confidence. It produces and feeds fear, and fear exaggerates and wants to control us. It's hard to be vulnerable in the face of those who have hurt us, consciously or unconsciously. But as we expose our wounded selves, God reveals Himself to us.

Even in the grave injustice of a fallen world, our hope rests fully on "the God who sees me" (Gen. 16:13). God sees you. God, the God who created all, who preserves, protects, and provides, is gracious and good. The God of Abraham, the Alpha and Omega, the beginning and end, the knower of all things … *that* God sees you.

I think the idea that *God* sees us scares a lot of people. But consider what Jesus, who was God, felt when He saw people. Matthew 9:36 comforts us with these words: "When he saw the crowds, *he had compassion* on them, because they were harassed and helpless, like sheep without a shepherd." Jesus, God in the flesh, saw. He saw each one, along with their hopes, dreams, and longings. And what did He feel about what He saw? Anger? Hatred? Repulsion? Shame? No, He felt compassion.

Imagine you are in that crowd. When He sees you, He has compassion for you, knowing that you are but dust. His affection for you is big. Being known by God is nothing to be afraid of; rather, it is something to be comforted by. You can rest secure, knowing you have a God who sees you.

You are not hidden from God. He sees you and how your life fits into His big picture. God sees *you*. He sees your intentions, your hard work, your diligence, your hope, your faith, your lack, your weaknesses, your perseverance, your gifts, your kindness, and your immense value.

## God Hears You

"Are you listening to me?" How often do we say that? Not many people feel refreshed by talking to a wall or being ignored. When we talk, we want the person we are talking to, to actually listen to us. And generally, listening means we have their attention.

Being a mom of six, I know that listening is exhausting. I have a quite unrealistic yet deep sense that I need to listen to each child all the time. And the children apparently have an intrinsic passion to be heard. All. The. Time. Even on the toilet: *"Mom!"* (Why can't they just wait a couple of minutes?)

But sometimes, if I'm intently focused on something, everything else can get drowned out. The cry of "She took my toy!" gets muffled because my own thoughts are so loud and all-encompassing. It's then that I hear one or another of my children demand, "Are you listening to me?"

In fact, this is a question most of us probably still ask today. We have a built-in need to be heard.

Scripture gives us an example, in the first chapter of 1 Samuel, about a bride who may have wondered if she was heard. It's likely that ever since she was a little girl, Hannah had wanted a baby. But when she grew up and became a wife, she found she couldn't have kids. Worse, not only was Hannah barren, but her husband had another wife—who wasn't barren. Hannah lived with someone who continually got what she wanted and rubbed her face in it. Perhaps Hannah heard biting comments that she didn't measure up or fit in and that she had no value, purpose, or anything to contribute to the world.

Could she have felt that God was punishing her or was mad at her? Maybe she was confused and full of self-pity. Perhaps she wondered why her husband still loved her even though she caused him embarrassment in the community. On top of it all, when she went to the place of worship to pour out her heart and plead with the Lord for a baby, her spiritual authority figure misunderstood and falsely accused her, assuming things about her that were not true. God seemed silent. Perhaps she felt He didn't hear her.

I imagine most of us have experienced these feelings. What did we do with our thoughts and feelings? Did we suppress them and hope they would go away? Did we spend our thought life complaining about them? Did we become bitter and hopeless? Did we end up with a critical outlook on life? Or did we turn to the Lord, as Hannah did? Did we bring our deepest desires to God and let Him give us rest?

Verses 10–11 tell us, "In her deep anguish Hannah prayed to the LORD, weeping bitterly. And she made a vow, saying, 'LORD Almighty, if you will only look on your servant's misery and remember me, and not forget your servant but give her a son, then

I will give him to the LORD for all the days of his life.'" Having a heart like Hannah's is not easy. She was vulnerable in telling God and others what her real desires were, even when they seemed distant and deaf.

Like Hannah, my husband, Austin, and I tried to have kids for many years. After five years of marriage, we were told we had unexplained infertility. We were unable to have kids, but the doctors didn't know why. During this time, I went to God, saying, "Please give us kids," but I never poured out my heart like Hannah, pleading with Him and confessing how badly I desired children. I stopped asking, just in case He said no. That way, I would have an out. If God didn't answer, I could claim, "I didn't really want that request anyway." I would "ask" as described in Matthew 7:7, but that was it. I would never seek or knock. I would never persist, as a way of protecting my heart. I would intellectually approach God but leave my real desires securely hidden.

This posture was driven by fear. I was so hesitant to trust my heart and desires to God for fear that He would let me down. I wouldn't come out from hiding for fear that God would ignore me. Or for fear that if He did hear, He would shrug me off and I would be crushed and feel uncared for. I was afraid that instead of experiencing His love for me, I would see Him ignore me and take no notice of me.

During this season, God began to teach me about taking my whole heart to Him instead of just sending up a quick "I'd really like a little boy, but if that's not what You want …" kind of prayer. The Lord asked me to be vulnerable and share my deepest desires with Him. He wanted me to come out of hiding and be heard. He asked me to trust Him with the outcome and to trust Him with my whole heart. So Austin and I started telling God that we really wanted to start a family, asking Him to give us a little boy. We even started praying for him by name: Asher Steven Krokos.

After two years of being real with my desires as I pleaded with God, He began to prompt us to consider adoption. A story on the radio, a divine encounter with an adopted man at a conference, a meeting with a grandma of a birth mom, and other seemingly "coincidental" events moved our hearts and minds to adjust to the possibility of adopting then instead of later, as we'd been considering.

The more we thought about it, the more realistic it seemed to take just one step. We didn't have to decide everything yet or even *if* we would adopt. We realized God just wanted us to take the next step. So we picked an agency and went to an information meeting.

The very next day, I received a surprise email from a friend. She knew a girl who was considering placing her soon-to-be-born baby for adoption. My friend asked if we were interested. We immediately said yes (although we weren't really expecting anything to happen). Two weeks later, however, we got to meet the birth mom and hear her story. We found out she wanted to adopt her baby to someone but that her husband was not in agreement. Just when we started to get our hopes up, they crumbled.

But a few weeks after that, the birth dad called and asked to meet us. Over lunch with the birth parents, Austin shared his testimony, and God used it to bring the birth dad to the point of saying yes. He told us he believed adoption was the right thing for this baby. The adoption was moving forward, and we couldn't believe it!

As we continued talking, the birth parents asked what names we were thinking about and whether we would consider their input. We had been praying for little Asher Steven for two years, so we were pretty set on the name. (Asher is a biblical name meaning "happy," and Steven is my dad's name.) The birth mom said, "If it's a girl, then I don't care what you name her. But I had a brother who died when I was little, and I've always said that if I ever had a boy, I wanted to name him after him."

Nervously, Austin asked, "What was your brother's name?"

"Steven," she replied.

I was floored. God had heard me. I had finally come out of hiding and vulnerably shared my heart with Him, and He had so obviously heard my pleas. The birth parents loved the name Asher Steven Krokos, which was incredible. So we became the parents of a boy with the initials A.S.K.—appropriate, since God had taught me to *ask* of Him, the One who hears.

When Jesus taught the disciples to pray, He emphasized persistence. He taught them to come to Him completely, not nonchalantly. God's desire is for us to bring our longings, passions, hopes, and expectations to Him, to connect with Him on the most real level of who we are. He wants to reveal Himself as the One who hears. But how can we perceive Him as such if we don't truly go to Him?

Being known by God requires that you share your experiences, thoughts, and feelings with Him—not because He doesn't already know them, but because a relationship deepens when you open up and share your heart. Sharing your heart with God strengthens your relationship with Him.

Look at Jesus: He poured out His heart vulnerably to the Father even in His weakest and most devastating time, knowing that God would hear Him. In the garden of Gethsemane, Jesus was so burdened that His sweat poured out like drops of blood. He knew what was to come. It was the worst possible scenario, and yet He didn't hide His desire for it to not go that way. He did say that if it wasn't His Father's will to avoid the cross, He would go through with it. But He didn't hide behind that, and He didn't fail to put His heart out there. He was vulnerable and shared His heart with His Father, and then He left the results up to God.

Jesus also shows us the heart of God by the way He sought to hear others. Consider the story of the paralyzed man at the pool of Bethesda, in John 5. When Jesus sees the man, He doesn't just fix his problem. He actually takes time to ask him, "What do you want?" Then He sits and listens to the guy. He hears his story about how the waters get churned up, yet someone always gets in before him. It's interesting to note that Jesus knew this superstition about the pool was not true, and yet He still sat and listened rather than rushing to correct. But then, after hearing him, Jesus acts. He heals. But allowing the man to voice his wants and frustrations mattered to Jesus.

This is true for you too. He would ask you the same thing. He wants you to bring your heart and desires to Him. He loves to hear you tell Him how you feel and what you want and all the things on your mind. Don't hide your heart from the One who wants to hear from you.

Don't hide your heart from the One who wants to hear from you.

# God Knows You

In analyzing 300,000 people in 148 studies, experts found that loneliness is associated with a 50 percent increase in mortality from any cause. This makes loneliness the equivalent of smoking fifteen cigarettes a day, and it makes it more deadly than obesity.[3] If we are not *known*, we can live in a city of two million and interact with dozens of people a day and still feel lonely.

The first step in being and feeling known is simple and yet powerful: for someone to know your name. Knowing someone's name moves you out of the "there's that random person" category into the "I know them" category. And when you speak using someone's name, you communicate respect and value. Being known is a core need of mankind. And how incredible it is that God goes out of His way to communicate to us that He knows us.

Every time I get a new Bible, I like to get a new version. It helps me avoid glossing over specific verses I have read many times, because a different translation brings new wording. I love the process of picking a new Bible. God meets me there every time.

So there I was, standing in front of a wall of Bibles at the Christian bookstore, asking the Lord to show me what Bible He wanted for me. I went back and forth, debating on the design and various versions.

There was one I wanted, but the wrinkles of fake leather on the cover were not spaced out in a way I liked. So I scanned the other covers until I saw one on the top shelf on the left-hand side. *That was it!* I pulled it down and took it out of the box. And there, sitting at the bottom of the box, was a little rectangular handwritten note that said "LAURA."

I have no idea how that happened. Had someone at the factory dropped it in by mistake? Had this Bible been ordered by some other Laura who never picked it up? Who had God used to put that note there, and how did He get that person to do it? I don't know, but I couldn't mistake that this was the Bible for me.

God, the One who breathed the stars into place, the One who holds all things together, knows your name.

Can you believe it? What a fun and generous God we have, who would orchestrate something like that. A reminder to me that He knows me. I was wowed by Him once again. God knows my name. And not just mine, but yours too!

Names hold deep significance. When someone uses your name, it carries weight. It says, "I care about you. I know you."

Names define us. And God, the One who breathed the stars into place, the One who holds all things together, knows *your name*. Take that in. He knows your *name*, the sum of everything about you. Not only does He see and hear you, He knows you. He is intimately acquainted with all your ways. Every tiny detail. He knows what you're passionate about and gravitate toward, and also what you hate and fear. He knows how you learn and how you receive.

The One who fashioned your cells, who wrote your DNA, who breathed the massive sun into the sky and created the killer whale and the octopus. The One who fashioned the star-nosed mole and the roly-poly, snowflakes and sequoias. The One whose story has been unfolding throughout history. The One around whom all of this revolves knows you. *He* knows you. He *knows* you. He knows *you*.

And did you know that this reality meets your soul's deepest need? To be fully known and still loved. And that very desire to be known is there because we are created in the image of God. We desire to be known because He desires to be known.

Remember Moses crying out to see and know God? As mentioned earlier, Max Lucado describes Moses's plea as asking this: "*Would you stun me with your strength? Numb me with your wisdom? Steal my breath with a brush of yours? A moment in the spray of the cataract of grace, a glimpse of your glory, God.*"[4] And God answers Moses with a resounding "Yes!" In Scripture, we continually see God taking initiative to be known, whether it be by putting on skin and becoming a man or by strategically placing the stars. What God made, He made to reveal Himself, to be known.

Though the world may applaud the things seen, the visible demonstrations of human glory, we have a God who celebrates the unseen, things like faithfulness and diligence. Our God sees and rewards good deeds done in secret (see Matt. 6:1–18).

You may feel uncelebrated, unnoticed, and unappreciated. But the reality is that, when you entrusted your life to Jesus, the angels celebrated over you (see Luke 15:10). You may feel unnoticed, but your mighty warrior sings over you (see Zeph. 3:17). You might not get applause and trophies from people, but your Father's audience is enough. You have His undivided attention. He is attentive to *you*.

The Lord has not overlooked you. He has not disregarded you. He knows exactly what He is doing. So often, we have to remind ourselves what's true: If the Lord is for me, who can be against me (see Rom. 8:31)? God radically loves you, and He is for you. You can rest. You are fully known and deeply loved. You are not hidden but rather seen, heard, and known. That, my friend, brings great rest to your soul.

# CONNECT WITH THE LORD

Watch the chapter 1 video now. Find the video using the QR code or link on page 22.

## God Sees, Hears, and Knows You

- In what ways do you feel unseen, unheard, and/or unknown?

- Look up the following passages, and write in your own words what they are saying:

    Job 37:16

    Psalm 139:1–4

    Psalm 147:5

Hebrews 4:13

1 John 3:20

- Which of these verses stands out to you? Why?

God is omniscient. *Omniscience* comes from two Latin words: *omni*, which means "all," and *scientia*, which means "knowledge." The omniscience of God means that He has perfect knowledge of all things, from tiny details to the end of time. He never needs to learn and will never forget. He knows all things past, present, and even in all possible futures. Let that sink in. All possible futures. There is nothing outside His realm of knowing.

His knowledge is absolute and unacquired. There was never a time when He didn't know something. It also means that God not only knows all things but also that He knows how to act on the knowledge He has, which is called wisdom. He knows exactly what to do, how to use everything He knows, and the full implications of every choice and action. God's knowledge has no limit.

- What thoughts and feelings do you have when thinking about how God knows ...

    Everything about you?

    Others in your life?

    Your future?

- How can you be more vulnerable in sharing your heart and desires with the Lord?

## Truth Chart

| | |
|---|---|
| • 1. Describe a recent time when you felt unseen, unheard, or unknown. | • 6. What is one way you can act on what is true? |
| • 2. How is it impacting your life: feelings, thoughts, choices? | • 5. If you believed God *knew all things*, how would it impact your wants and actions? |
| • 3. What does it show that you believe about God? | • 4. If you believed God *knew all things*, how would it impact your feelings? |

# Chapter 2

# You Are Wanted

Not long ago, my husband and I moved our six kids to a small town to better serve our ministry, which has its headquarters in that small town. Leaving was hard, as I had just developed some precious friendships after my heart had been longing to connect with other women.

Not long after getting settled, I found some people to love, serve, and sacrifice for. I gave my heart, time, and resources to this small group of moms and kids. A short time later, we went through a traumatic season of our kids dealing with mental and physical illnesses. I leaned into these new friendships, and many loved us well.

However, some did not. When some of these people felt the pain and fear the illnesses caused, they rejected us and shunned us. Someone I considered a friend told her kids they were not allowed to be friends with mine.

I was crushed and felt abandoned. I was wounded, so I shut myself up inside a shell of self-protection. The pain of rejection and my own fear led to isolating myself, which left me vulnerable to the lie of the Enemy: that no one wanted to be around me or my kids.

That lie sank deeper as I held onto it. I would not invite people over, believing no one would want to come. I stopped using my gifts to serve, as I truly believed I was unwanted.

Perhaps you've been wounded like me. Perhaps on a much grander scale than a friend abandoning you. Maybe it was a parent or a spouse. Chances are, you've felt the sting of rejection, and perhaps it has led to not trusting people. Perhaps it's left you longing for acceptance. Rejection is one of the most powerful tools of the Enemy. And Jesus wants to dismantle its power over us.

We are created with a longing to be wanted. We want to be accepted, to fit in, to feel like we belong. It's why rejection stings so much. And now, with daily access to social media and photos of people around us, we get even more opportunities to see the places where we weren't invited or included, which can leave us feeling unwanted and alone.

The deceiver loves to take advantage of these moments by spewing his lies. As soon as you feel that sting of being unwanted, he starts whispering things like, "You're too much trouble for them," "You're not _____ enough," and "No one really wants to be around you." If you succumb to a lie, it's "Battle over. One point for the Enemy."

But trying to fight these lies in the wrong way leads us down a failing path as well. If we try to push back against these lies with human-centered theology that says, "You are too brave, pretty, strong" (or whatever else you'd fill in the blank with), we end up only shifting the battleground. Maybe the pain of rejection settles a bit, but bitterness grows as the finger of accusation comes up. The lies about "them" now start: "I *am* strong enough—it's just that *they* can't handle *me*" or "I *am* good enough—they just can't see it." It's basically putting ourselves up and putting others down as a way to feel wanted. It's an effort to make ourselves believe we are better than them in order to avoid the pain of not being wanted.

There's a better way to fight the Enemy's lies: with the double-edged sword, the Word of God (see Eph. 6:17). This means remembering and believing what God says is true about us and them. This battle looks different from the "I am too" argument. It recognizes the pain of feeling left out. And it also recognizes the lie the Enemy whispers of "You're not _____ enough." But it shouts back, "I may not be, but Jesus is."

Rejection is one of
the most powerful
tools of the Enemy.

The reality is that we might *not* actually be strong enough, smart enough, good enough, friendly enough, skinny enough, pretty enough, and on and on. But Jesus is enough. And He is our sufficiency. The goal isn't to tell ourselves how good we are so we can feel wanted. The goal is to recognize that we already *are* deeply and passionately wanted by the most important One of all.

Much as we might want it to, being wanted by people will never give us the satisfaction our souls crave. Let that sink in. Even if we were wanted by the people we most want to want us, it wouldn't satisfy. People's affections change, and we are a flaky bunch, us humans. You can see it all over Scripture. One moment, they love Peter, and the next, they're trying to kill him (see Acts 3–4). One moment, they're yelling, "Hosanna!" to Jesus as He rides into Jerusalem on a donkey; only a few days later, they're yelling, "Crucify Him!" (see Matt. 21; 27).

Trying to satisfy our souls' cravings to be wanted with anything besides Jesus is like digging in the desert hoping to find water. Living to get approval, acceptance, adoration, and admiration from others is like going to a dry well. Recognizing and deeply understanding that we are wanted by God is the only way our souls will be fulfilled and satisfied.

Have you ever noticed how often we make decisions based on being wanted? Or have you thought about how often you seek to fulfill your longing to be wanted? Do you pursue it by people-pleasing, as we see in Galatians 1:10? "Am I now trying to win the approval of human beings, or of God? Or am I trying to please people? If I were still trying to please people, I would not be a servant of Christ."

If I were to guess how often I think about being wanted, I would say it's probably daily. When I walk into a room, I want someone to be interested in talking to me. When I see something on social media I wasn't invited to, I wish I had been. And the list goes on. This longing is normal. But it becomes dangerous when we try to get that longing satisfied in places other than Jesus. That's called idolatry.

Idolatry is craving or being satisfied by anything we treasure more than God. It is a disordered love or desire. And the thing about idols is that they demand sacrifices.

When we idolize being wanted, the sacrifice often becomes the very person we wish would want us back. You suck the life out of him or her and the relationship. Rather than seeing that person as someone God put in your life to love and serve, you see that person as someone to serve *you*.

For example, say I'm working on something important, and my kiddos come in demanding my attention. In my impatience I yell at them. My idol of time was just exposed as I sacrificed my kids' hearts on the altar. This can happen with all sorts of things, like comfort, convenience, pleasure, and so on.

God goes to great lengths to help us turn away from idols and to Him. He is the only one worthy of our full reliance. He will graciously allow our people idols to fall short and to be exposed as unworthy of our worship.

However, God is not calling us to squish down our desire to be wanted and enjoyed. Rather, He is calling us to find its fulfillment in Him. We can delight ourselves in Him because He first greatly delights in us. We will either cling to our unfulfilling idols or cling to the Lover of our souls.

## God Loves You

You've heard the familiar refrain before: "Jesus loves you." It's a powerful sentence, yet when people hear it, they often feel nothing. Sometimes, information that stays only in our intellect becomes bland. It's not until we chew on it, spending time really processing and internalizing it, that it comes to life. Other times, certain words get overused and lose their impact. Maybe this phrase has lost its significance in your heart?

Perhaps that's because *love* is an overused word in our society. I love ice cream. I love puppies. I love my husband. They all get lumped into the same category. In ancient Greek, there were different words for different types of love. There was a word for the love you had for things, the love you had for family, the love you felt for a friend, the love you experienced in romantic attraction, and so on.

But the biggie type of love is the one referred to by the Greek word *agape*. This is the one God loves us with. Agape love is the unconditional, do-what's-in-another's-best-interest type of love. We see it in John 3:16: "God so loved the world that he gave his one and only Son." This love is more than an emotion—it is a choice to do what's in the best interest of someone else. Agape love is putting the interests of others ahead of yourself. It's not based on attraction but is an act of the will. God will always choose to do what's best for you.

His love for you is not based on anything you do or don't do. His love for you is perfect and will never fail. He can never love you less or more. God's love is unconditional because He is incapable of not loving you perfectly. Sometimes we won't understand God's love and why He demonstrated His love in one way and not another. But that doesn't mean it's not love. Our understanding of love doesn't define it.

It's not just that God loves you—God also *enjoys* you.

Does that hit you differently, as it does me? *Enjoy* means to "take pleasure or satisfaction in the possession or experience of; to feel or perceive with pleasure; to be delighted with."[1]

This makes me think of my daughter Willow. Though at the time I am writing this she is a tiny seven-year-old, she has a larger-than-life personality. Her exuberance lights up a room. Wherever she goes, she fills the room with smiles. Sometimes I just stare at her because she is a delight. I take pleasure in her, in how she says things and does things, even her little quirky things. It's not uncommon for people to giggle at what she says and does. One time, she was very upset that people were laughing at her. I had to explain that she was just so cute that she made people smile so big that a giggle came out.

Jesus takes pleasure in you the same way. I think you may just bring a smile to Him that is so big, He has to giggle. Truly, the Lord takes pleasure in you.

I enjoy painting. I always get a sense of pleasure when I have completed a project. I believe many artists take pleasure in the work of their hands: from architects, who get to see their buildings completed, to seamstresses delighting in their final

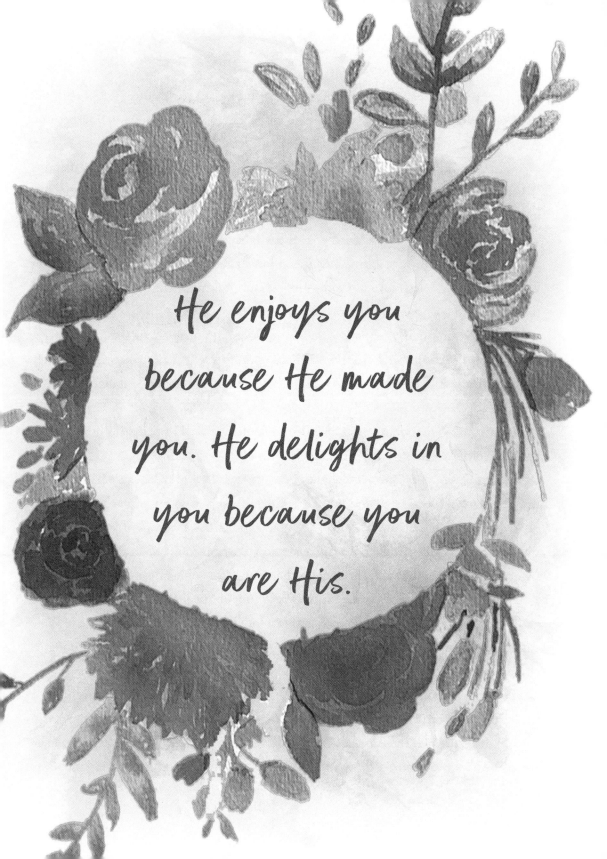

He enjoys you
because He made
you. He delights in
you because you
are His.

products. In the same way, the Maker delights in you just as a potter delights in the work of his hands. He enjoys you because He made you. He delights in you because you are His.

What would you do if someone told you to act out the emotion of delight? What movements would you use? Perhaps you'd smile, or maybe you'd make big arm motions. You might dance or jump. Zephaniah 3:17 describes it in a pretty incredible way: "The LORD your God is with you, the Mighty Warrior who saves. He will take great delight in you; in his love he will no longer rebuke you, but will rejoice over you with singing." This love of God—the pleasure-taking, delighting, rejoicing love of God over you—looks big, extravagant, and loud.

Often, I think many Christians feel as if God is ho-hum about them or that He is an unfeeling, distant dictator. Perhaps some think He just puts up with or barely tolerates them. And yet, here we see Him dancing out of delight, singing because of His love.

Isaiah 62:3–5 describes God's delight and rejoicing over His people as how a bridegroom rejoices over his bride: "My Delight is in Her" (v. 4 HCSB).

Psalm 37:23 (NLT) says He delights in every detail of your life. My friend, every detail! How God sees detail and how we see detail are just not even on the same playing field. God sees each atom. And yet, God delights in every *detail* of your life. He is mindful of every tiny detail about you, even down to how many hairs are on your head (which, I might point out, is continually changing—for some faster than for others).

Psalm 139:17–18 says a pretty incredible thing about just how mindful He is of you: "How precious to me are your thoughts, God! How vast is the sum of them! Were I to count them, they would outnumber the grains of sand." God has more thoughts about you than there are little pieces of sand on the shore.

Let's think about that a second to get the full impact. Have you ever picked up a pinch of sand and tried to count the grains? It's quite shocking how many grains are in a pinch. It's estimated there are about a thousand. If you were to fill a tablespoon, there would be about a hundred thousand, and there are about a million grains in a cup.

That's a ton of grains of sand, and yet, it is only one cup. Can you imagine how many grains are on the beaches of all the oceans? "Researchers estimate there are 7.5 quintillion grains of sand on the Earth's beaches. (That's 7,500,000,000,000,000,000!)"[2]

The God who knows just how many grains of sand there are on the earth has even more thoughts than that toward you. I wouldn't call that a distant God who merely tolerates you. You are His treasure. You are valuable and precious to Him. You are loved. First Peter 5:7 declares that God "cares for you affectionately and cares about you watchfully" (AMPC).

You may wonder how your behavior fits in. Does He love you less when you act like a nincompoop? Is His desire for you less when you don't perform in certain ways or when you totally fail Him? No. God looks at His kiddos (which, I need to point out, is not everyone, but we'll talk about this more in the next chapter) through the lens of Jesus' imputed righteousness. That means Jesus' righteousness is put on you when you surrender your life to Him. It means God counts you perfect in Christ, not because you are but because Jesus is, and He is standing in front of you as you stand before the Father.

None of your sin—past, present, or future—can be seen, because it is covered by Jesus' perfection. For those who have put their trust in Jesus, His righteousness has been transferred to them.

God also sees you becoming what you already are in Christ. Do you remember how I said that God loves and delights in you the way a groom delights in his bride? And then I talked about how God thinks about you a whole gobful. That's like a groom who can't stop thinking about his bride.

But there's something else grooms do that gives us a picture of God's love for you: grooms brag about their brides. Did you know that God brags about you? Remember Job's story? It's both super sad and overwhelmingly redemptive. It all started with God bragging about a guy He loved.

In Job 1:8, Satan approaches the throne and *God says*, "Have you considered my servant Job, that there is none like him on the earth, a blameless and upright man, who

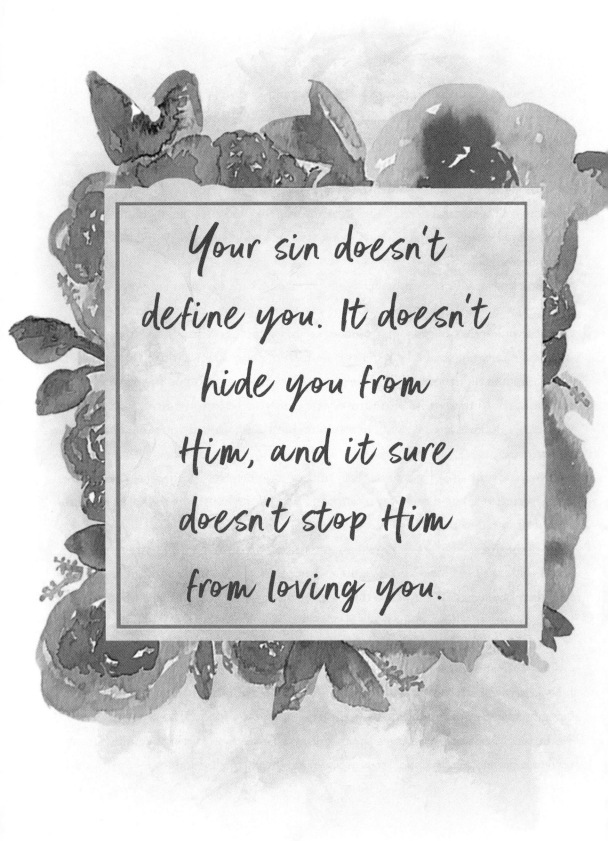

Your sin doesn't define you. It doesn't hide you from Him, and it sure doesn't stop Him from loving you.

fears God and turns away from evil?" (ESV). God was bragging about Job and how well he loved Him. That's mind-blowing.

There are also times when we see Jesus, who was God in the flesh, bragging about people. He especially liked to brag about their faith. One time, He even bragged about a former prostitute. The story goes like this: Simon the Pharisee, a religious leader, invited Jesus to his house, but he didn't do the customary things you'd do to honor a guest. In modern times, those practices would be equivalent to taking someone's jacket and offering him a drink. But Simon didn't do any of it.

Then a lady who had been rescued and forgiven for a lot enters the story. She is crying, and I speculate that this is because of how Jesus, her forgiver, is being treated. She approaches Him and begins to wipe His feet with her hair and precious oil, the most valuable possession she had. When Simon and the other religious leaders start whispering and gossiping about Jesus and the lady, the Lord pipes up and starts publicly bragging about her. It's beautiful.

You can read her story in Luke 7:36–50. Jesus looks right at Simon and says, "I have something to say to you" (v. 40 ESV). He proceeds to tell him a parable about two debtors and how the one who was forgiven more, loves more. In front of everyone, He calls Simon out for his attitude, then brags about the woman.

> Then turning toward the woman he said to Simon, "Do you see this woman? I entered your house; you gave me no water for my feet, but she has wet my feet with her tears and wiped them with her hair. You gave me no kiss, but from the time I came in she has not ceased to kiss my feet. You did not anoint my head with oil, but she has anointed my feet with ointment. Therefore I tell you, her sins, which are many, are forgiven—for she loved much. But he who is forgiven little, loves little." And he said to her, "Your sins are forgiven." (vv. 44–48 ESV)

This lady was previously known by her sin. But God rescued her, and now He saw her through the perfection of Jesus. It was hard for people to see but easy for Jesus to brag about.

Your sin is the same way. Your sin doesn't define you. It doesn't hide you from Him, and it sure doesn't stop Him from loving you. Jesus reveals the heart of the Father in His response to the forgiven woman. He didn't shun her—He praised her. He wasn't embarrassed to be around her. He drew her in and spoke to her, wanting to be in her presence.

He wants to be with you too. Psalm 23 gives us an incredible visual of how much God loves you and wants to spend time with you. In ancient times, if the host kept refilling the guest's cup, it was a way of showing that the guest was invited to stay longer. When the host would allow the cup to empty, it was a way of saying it was time for the guest to leave.

When the psalmist says, "My cup overflows" (v. 5), he is saying that God wanted to be with him. The Lord didn't want him to leave but rather wanted to spend time with him. So it is with Jesus' love for you. And it's not only in this life that He wants time with you. He has made it possible for a finite, mortal person—once separated from Him by sin—to now live with Him for eternity. He loves you so much that He wants to spend forever with you.

In every way you can receive it, God demonstrates His abounding love for you. God not only wants you but also deeply loves and enjoys you. And as a result, He will faithfully pursue you.

> I pray that out of his glorious riches he may strengthen you with power through his Spirit in your inner being, so that Christ may dwell in your hearts through faith. And I pray that you, being rooted and established in love, may have power, together with all the Lord's holy people, to grasp how wide and long and high and deep is the love of Christ, and to know this love that surpasses knowledge—that you may be filled to the measure of all the fullness of God. (Eph. 3:16–19)

This God who is smitten with you, who thinks about you more times than there are grains of sand on the shore, pursues you.

# God Pursues You

When you think of pursuit, what do you imagine? Perhaps a young man buying gifts, calling and sending texts, asking to spend time with the young lady he loves.

One of my children is interested in a girl, and he thinks about her often. As he was unloading the dishwasher one day, he told me about how at youth group he had asked someone who seemed left out to be his partner in a game. The girl he liked said, "No, you're *my* partner." He asked me if maybe he had hurt her feelings by asking the other kid to be his partner instead of her. My heart swelled to hear that my boy is thinking of others.

But isn't thinking of someone the first step in pursuit? How can you pursue someone if you don't give him or her any thought? We've already established how often God thinks about you: a lot. So what does He do with those thoughts? Nothing? No way. Our God is an active, get-things-done type of God. He does not just sit and think about doing what's best for you—He does it. His love and pursuit go hand in hand. This God who is smitten with you, who thinks about you more times than there are grains of sand on the shore, pursues you.

The story of Hosea and Gomer always breaks my heart. It's an Old Testament story of a man whose job it was to tell people about God. But God's way of telling people about Himself was to *show* them, to give them a live illustration. And this was no drawing on a dry-erase board or PowerPoint presentation. This demonstration was to have the prophet Hosea take a prostitute for a wife, to pursue and love her with everything he had, only to watch her turn to other lovers.

It is such a great picture of how God took an unfaithful bride (the people of Israel) and relentlessly pursued her regardless of her behavior. The book of Hosea is a picture of how God gave His heart completely to those who would utterly reject Him. How often we are like Gomer, an ungrateful adulteress, when it comes to God. Like Gomer, we look to other things to find our approval, acceptance, adoration, and admiration.

By contrast, the Song of Solomon (another Old Testament book called by some translations the Song of Songs) paints a picture of a bride and groom who are faithful. The book is the story of a young man romancing a girl through poems, unleashing his affection, and committing to wooing her—along with the bride's response to his pursuit. Like the book of Hosea, Song of Solomon is a metaphor for God's pursuit of us.

The pursuit of God is seen in other places too, like Jeremiah 32:40–41, where God says, "I will never stop doing good to them, and I will inspire them to fear me, so that they will never turn away from me. I will rejoice in doing them good and will assuredly plant them in this land with all my heart and soul." He will never stop doing good to you. What an incredible pursuit!

One time, I was in a Christian bookstore looking at the Bible studies. I couldn't decide which one I wanted to do, and I noticed one I hadn't seen before. I picked it up and thumbed through it. It sparked my interest. Just then, the lady working at the store walked up to me and said, "Excuse me. You have just received a phone call. The author of that study just called and said the Lord told him someone was looking at his Bible study and to tell them that God loved them." I stood there in shock, unable to answer. What in the world? I had no idea how to respond, but I did know that God wanted me to know He loved and pursued me. (And of course, I bought that study.)

Maybe you can agree with me that God pursues people, but perhaps you're less certain that He pursues *you*. After all, He has not exactly shown up on your doorstep with flowers. And yet His pursuit of you began before you were even born. Acts 17:26–27 tells us that He picked the exact place and time period that you would be born in order for you to have the best chance of pursuing Him back.

He has pursued you, wooing you to notice Him and depend on Him. Not only has He put people in your life to show you what He is like, but He has also used His creation to woo you, showing you His attributes, power, and nature (see Rom. 1:20). He uses His creation, His people, and even your circumstances to pursue you. But the chances are good that you might not recognize or know them as pursuit.

Sometimes, He allows hard, lonely seasons in our lives to get us to pursue Him. I like how Steve DeWitt says it when talking about loneliness:

> Yet even the best moments of marriage and parenting and friendship always lack something; the moment of harmony passes too quickly. The warm feelings of care slip away. Human relationships ebb and flow. Even at their best, we sense that something is missing.…
>
> We should be glad to realize that the best of this life leaves us wanting something more, longer, and better. As wonderful as these earthly gifts are, the fact that they don't satisfy makes God's promises to fully satisfy us forever even more astounding.… Every loneliness on earth is an internal confirmation that our greatest relational joys lie ahead of us. Absence should make the heart look forward.[3]

Hard, lonely things that we experience are invitations to pursue Him back. In Matthew 15, we meet a Canaanite mom who seeks Jesus. Because she has a child who is mentally tormented, the whole family is desperate. She seeks Jesus, begging Him to heal her daughter. What does Jesus do? He ignores her! Verse 23 says, "He did not say a word to her" (HCSB). How crazy is that? The disciples, annoyed at her, ask Jesus to send her away. (How often do we want the same thing when we're sick of dealing with something? *Just make it/them go away already.*") But then He makes a comment to push her to keep seeking Him: "I was sent only to the lost sheep of the house of Israel" (v. 24 HCSB).

Will she keep pursuing Him? She does, kneeling before Him, no less. And then He makes another comment to woo her: "It isn't right to take the children's bread and throw it to their dogs" (v. 26 HCSB). Just for some context: this was not a derogatory term. As Warren Wiersbe explains it,

Jesus did not call her a "dog" the way the Pharisees would have addressed a Gentile. The Greek word means "a little pet dog" and not the filthy curs that ran the streets and ate the garbage.… Jesus was not playing games with the woman, nor was he trying to make the situation more difficult. He was drawing out of her a growing response of faith.[4]

She pursues Him still, and the most beautiful thing happens as a result! She persists and keeps pleading because … what else is there? He alone has life. He is her only hope. Likely (as we still see today), her family's friends don't want to be around them. Likely, she's heard this "make her go away" comment time and time again. This mama is exhausted, discouraged, and wounded. And yet she's not going anywhere until Jesus answers her desperate call for rescue. Her love for her kiddo drives her to Jesus, where her faith can grow stronger.

And He does rescue. He responds to her pursuit of Him. After all, He is the One who wooed her. He not only answers her but ends up praising her faith. Jesus, God, Creator, and Sustainer praises her faith: "'Woman, your faith is great. Let it be done for you as you want.' And from that moment her daughter was cured" (v. 28 HCSB).

The pain God allows has purpose, and often that purpose is to strengthen our faith. But of course! How else will our faith get strong? Just like muscles, faith grows only when it's torn, stretched to the point of breaking, so it can heal back stronger.

God is pursuing you, and like little kids playing chase, He is wooing you to pursue Him back. Will you keep pursuing and seeking Him, even when others want you to go away? Even when the pain is deep and it seems like even Jesus Himself isn't listening? I pray you do. There is great reward.

God won't give up pursuing you. He will continue to woo your heart even in ways you might not recognize as pursuit. He whispers and woos until we answer. Louie Giglio says it this way: "The God who creates everything and needs nothing, pursues you. Don't let anyone sell you less worth than that."[5]

In Psalm 63:3, David describes the pursuing love of God as "better than life." No one and nothing else can satisfy our longing to be loved like God loves. We will always come up wanting when we look to anyone or anything else to find God's kind of love.

God wants you, loves you, and will continually pursue you. Jesus took on the rejection of people that we might be accepted by His Father. Believing that you are accepted by Him drowns out the rejection of people.

Let God quiet you with His love today. Let His delight in you free you from needing to prove yourself or outperform everyone else.

# CONNECT WITH THE LORD

Watch the chapter 2 video now. Find the video using the QR code or link on page 22.

## God Wants, Loves, and Pursues You

• How would you describe the love God has for you? What is His love based on?

• How have you seen the pursuing love of God in your life?

• If you deeply believed God enjoyed you, how would that change your life?

• How do you seek to fulfill your longing to be wanted?

• What thoughts and feelings surface when considering that God enjoys you?

• How could knowing that God delights in you bring freedom?

• Look up the following passages, and write in your own words what they are saying:

Matthew 23:37

John 3:16–17

Romans 5:8

Romans 8:35, 37–39

Ephesians 2:4–5

Ephesians 3:18–19

• What does Luke 15:3–10 teach about the pursuit of God?

• Which of these verses stands out to you the most? Why?

## Truth Chart

| | |
|---|---|
| • 1. In what ways have you recently felt unwanted, unloved, or disregarded? | • 6. What is one way you can act on what is true? |
| • 2. How is it impacting your life: feelings, thoughts, choices? | • 5. If you believed God *loved, wanted, and pursued you,* how would it impact your wants and actions? |
| • 3. What does it show that you believe about God? | • 4. If you believed God *loved, wanted, and pursued you,* how would it impact your feelings? |

In our performance-based world, relationships often depend on how well someone behaves, and love is given only when earned. But this is the very opposite of God's love for us. We are secure because of Jesus' performance, which has been credited to our account.

From the beginning, we can see God wanting, loving, pursuing, and delighting in us. Genesis 1:26 and 31 tell us, "God said, 'Let us make mankind in our image, in our likeness....' God saw all that he had made, and it was very good." Much confusion has arisen over God's reference to Himself as "us" in this passage. But remember, God is a Trinity: Father, Son, and Holy Spirit. It's proper to think of God as both singular and plural. The Hebrew word used here for "God" is *Elohim*, the plural form of *El*, which you may be familiar with in names like El Shaddai or Beth-El.

By choosing to use *Elohim* here, Moses is emphasizing the plural nature of God. His perfect fellowship chose to create us. He had no need of us; He wasn't lonely or bored. He just chose to widen His circle of delight and let us share in His fellowship. He needed nothing, and yet He gave everything—because He is a delighting God.

Chapter 3

# You Are Not Hopeless

At four years old, Stephanie was loaded onto a Korean train by her mother and sent away. When she got off at her destination, no one met her, and she would wait at the station day after day while weeping for her mom. For the next three years, she endured things no child should ever experience as she tried to survive.

One time she and another little girl were thrown into an abandoned building infested with rats. Stephanie had learned during her time on the streets to keep kicking her feet when resting near rats, because otherwise they would bite her toes. So when she saw the rats coming, she kept repeating this advice to the girl. But the girl was too sick to fight them off, and the rats ended up killing her. Stephanie escaped back onto the streets.

With all hope gone, Stephanie one day found herself looking up into a lady's blue eyes. This woman was a foreign nurse in Korea who would search for abandoned babies, nurse them to health, and take them to an orphanage. This particular day, she had passed near a garbage alley, a way she never went. As she walked past a pile of trash, she heard a groan. When she investigated, she saw Stephanie.

The nurse thought Stephanie was too sick and young to survive, but as she stood to walk away, she felt like her legs were cement and she couldn't move. Then she heard an invisible voice say, "She is Mine." So she picked up the girl, who was covered with

Suffering paves the way
for God's character to
be put on display.

sores, lice, and filth, and became a part of God's rescue story for Stephanie. Eventually, a missionary couple adopted her from the orphanage.

Today, Stephanie is passionate about being a voice for the 217 million orphans of the world. You can read her detailed account in her book, *She Is Mine*.[1]

There is no shortage of painful stories in this life. I'm sure that if you haven't gone through heart-wrenching pain yourself, you know someone who has. You don't have to look far to have your heart ripped out by stories of what people in this world are enduring. And yet suffering paves the way for God's character to be put on display. Hearing stories of redemption gives us confidence to walk through all kinds of difficulties without being shaken. When we view God as bigger than our problems and our present suffering, we find a quiet confidence replacing fear and anxiety.

No matter what you or the people in your life are facing—whether not being able to have kids; not getting the job, role, or opportunity you wanted; or life not turning out the way you had always imagined—there is hope because of who God is: the rescuer, redeemer, and restorer.

> But now, this is what the LORD says—
>> he who created you, Jacob,
>> he who formed you, Israel:
> "Do not fear, for I have redeemed you;
>> I have summoned you by name; *you are mine.*
> When you pass through the waters,
>> I will be with you;
> and when you pass through the rivers,
>> they will not sweep over you.
> When you walk through the fire,
>> you will not be burned;
>> the flames will not set you ablaze.
> For I am the LORD your God,
>> the Holy One of Israel, your Savior." (Isa. 43:1–3)

# God Rescues

In our family, when we get Amber Alerts, we pray together. A child getting kidnapped is one of those gut punches where you ache for whoever lost their kid, not being able to imagine what that would be like.

A few years ago, I read that the majority of girls who are taken and trafficked were first pursued by someone online. The article explained that it used to be that girls were often picked up at bus stops. That's when a memory hit me. When I was in junior high, I asked my parents if I could spend the night at a friend's house. They said yes, but I don't think I told them that I didn't have a way to get there and that I would need to ride the bus. As I was sitting at the bus stop, terrified because I had never ridden the big-city public transportation in my eleven years of life, a scary old man in a beat-up car pulled up and asked me if I wanted a ride.

He was even scarier than the bus, so I was quick to say no. And, of course, I knew not to get in a car with a stranger. But not a minute or two later, another guy drove up in a shiny, clean pickup truck. He was young and seemed nice. He reminded me of the dad of the kids I babysat. He asked me if I wanted a ride. He seemed a whole lot safer than the bus, so I hesitated.

I knew not to get in the car, but he seemed so nice, and I was so scared to ride the bus. He asked me where I was going, and I told him Ken Caryl, a suburb of Denver. He said that was exactly where he was headed. I was naively shocked, as it was forty minutes away. I never was a big rule follower, and at eleven, my ability to reason apparently wasn't very strong, so I got in. *I got in the car with a stranger!*

It wasn't very long into our drive that he asked me about boyfriends, and we talked about that almost the entire way. When we were close to my friend's house, it finally kicked in that I probably shouldn't show him where my friend lived, so I directed him to her neighborhood clubhouse. When we were close to arriving, he asked me if I wanted to go get a drink. An odd question for a junior high kid. I said no, but he asked again and again. After the fourth time, I just got out of the car and walked to my friend's house, not realizing the danger I'd been in, and I never said anything to anyone.

God had rescued me, and I didn't realize it until thirty years later.

Our Lord rescues. He goes into hidden places and brings people out of the dark and into the light.

We can be ignorant of the ways the Lord has rescued us, but that doesn't mean it hasn't happened. Maybe our ignorance is because we honestly didn't know, as had happened to me. Maybe it's because what we endured was hard and it didn't *feel* like He rescued. Maybe it's because the rescue hasn't come yet. Or maybe it's because we have a small view of what His rescue looks like or what we've been rescued from.

Stories like Stephanie's can perhaps lead us to think our own stories are not that big of a deal. But God rescues us from all sorts of things: relationships, addictions, lies, circumstances, and even ourselves.

Even if we have a low view of ourselves, as we often are our own worst critics, at the same time we can think we aren't that bad. But let's see how we measure up against God's standard. Have you ever lied? I have. What does that make us? Liars. Have you ever stolen something, regardless of value? I have. What does that make us? Thieves. Have you ever made anything more important than God? I have. That makes us idolaters. So by our own admission, we are lying, stealing idolaters at heart. And that's only three of His Ten Commandments.

God tells us there's a penalty for people who have done these types of things, these things called sin: separation from Him for all eternity. The punishment is hell, which is a hard word to say these days. You and I rightly deserve hell. Christian hip-hop artist Lecrae says it this way: "If we fought for our rights, we'd be in hell tonight."[2] It is utterly hopeless to think we could ever be perfect or measure up to God's standard. Anyway, we've already biffed it.

But God …

These two incredible words bring hope. You are not hopeless. It's true that a foe had his grip on you, *but God* came to your aid. A king gave His life in exchange for yours.

He took the punishment you deserved, the payment of death and eternal separation, to make you a citizen of heaven. That, my friend, is a radical story of rescue.

Maybe our stories don't feel like they are that powerful because we are not convinced we truly deserve hell. But we do. Even if we're not as bad as some others, we still fall short of God's standard: perfection. But if you have admitted your guilt to God and surrendered your life to Him, He has rescued you. The One who fashioned your cells rescued you from an eternity of suffering. And get this: He even knew you'd choose other things over Him. He knew you'd sin, and He made you anyway, with all your wonderful cells and atoms. He knew He would "wrath Himself" on your behalf.* You do have a very powerful story.

Hell is one of those topics no one wants to talk about. But really, if you knew how bad it was and you thought someone was going there after death, how much would you have to hate that person to not give a warning—and all because it's a little uncomfortable to talk about?

So since it's likely we don't have a very accurate view of hell, let's start with what the Bible says about it. Jesus told a story that takes place there. Let's take a look.

> ¹⁹There was a rich man who was dressed in purple and fine linen and lived in luxury every day. ²⁰At his gate was laid a beggar named Lazarus, covered with sores ²¹and longing to eat what fell from the rich man's table. Even the dogs came and licked his sores.
>
> ²²The time came when the beggar died and the angels carried him to Abraham's side. The rich man also died and was buried. ²³In Hades, where he was in torment, he looked up and saw Abraham far away, with Lazarus by his side. ²⁴So he called to him, "Father Abraham, have pity on me and send Lazarus to dip the tip of his finger in water and cool my tongue, because I am in agony in this fire."

---

\* God chose to take His own wrath out on Himself so that we wouldn't experience it. See Romans 5:9.

$^{25}$But Abraham replied, "Son, remember that in your lifetime you received your good things, while Lazarus received bad things, but now he is comforted here and you are in agony. $^{26}$And besides all this, between us and you a great chasm has been set in place, so that those who want to go from here to you cannot, nor can anyone cross over from there to us."

$^{27}$He answered, "Then I beg you, father, send Lazarus to my family, $^{28}$for I have five brothers. Let him warn them, so that they will not also come to this place of torment."

$^{29}$Abraham replied, "They have Moses and the Prophets; let them listen to them."

$^{30}$"No, father Abraham," he said, "but if someone from the dead goes to them, they will repent."

$^{31}$He said to him, "If they do not listen to Moses and the Prophets, they will not be convinced even if someone rises from the dead." (Luke 16:19–31)

Here are nineteen things we see about hell from this story:

1. The rich man was tormented in hell (v. 23).
2. He looked and saw far away, showing that in hell there is physical sight (v. 23).
3. He saw even into heaven (v. 23).
4. He recognized people, even people he had only heard about (such as Abraham, v. 23).
5. He called out, meaning that in hell he had both a voice and a longing (v. 24).
6. He experienced such agony that he wanted relief from any source (v. 24).

7.  He retained the ability to hope and to cry out for help (e.g., asking for Lazarus to give him even just a drop, v. 24).

8.  He wanted pity (v. 24).

9.  He was in agony (v. 24).

10. He had a tongue, showing that he retained a physical body that could suffer torment (v. 24).

11. He remembered his life on earth (v. 25).

12. His agony was contrasted with comfort, indicating that he would never be comforted (v. 25).

13. There was a separation between paradise and hell, a separation that can never be bridged (v. 26).

14. He remembered his family and still cared for them (v. 27).

15. His desire was for none of his loved ones to end up in hell (v. 27–28).

16. He had thoughts, opinions, and ideas but could do nothing about them (v. 30).

17. He understood that he deserved to be in hell (v. 30).

18. He was alone.

19. He experienced unending regret.[3]

The Bible uses some pretty intense words to describe hell: *fire* (Matt. 5:22), *fiery oven* (Ps. 21:9 NKJV), *judgment by fire* (Amos 7:4), *eternal destruction* (2 Thess. 1:9 ESV), *unquenchable fire* (Mark 9:43–48 ESV), *gloomy darkness* (2 Pet. 2:4 ESV), *darkness* (Matt. 25:30), *eternal fire* (Matt. 25:41), *torment* (Luke 16:23), *weeping* (Matt. 8:12), *gnashing of teeth* (Matt. 13:42), *fiery lake* (Rev. 20:15 NLT), *condemned* (Matt. 12:36–37), and *destruction* (Phil. 1:28 ESV). Yikes! So basically, it's going to be awful. Really awful. Scripture also tells us what the people in hell will be going through: torment with no rest day and night (Rev. 14:11).

You and I deserve hell because we haven't lived perfect lives. Everyone deserves hell except Jesus, who was 100 percent man and 100 percent God, who put on skin and came to live the perfect life we couldn't. Then He died, paying the penalty we rightly deserved. He rose from the dead, proving He was God and the only one able to conquer death and forgive us.

His life, death, and resurrection allow us to be offered a pardon from hell as a free gift. Have you received that gift from Him? Or are you hoping your guilt will somehow be covered up by good things you do? It is a radical rescue that the perfect God wrathed Himself so we might receive forgiveness! If we receive His forgiveness, we will never become inhabitants of hell … ever … no matter what.

When you have been rescued by the God who shaped your kidneys, what can shake you? If He knew all your flaws and failures even before you were born and He still chose to make and love you anyway, surely nothing you do can keep Him from rescuing you, taking you by your right hand, and leading you. Your story is a rescue story.

Or perhaps your story doesn't seem like a rescue because it's not yet. Because you haven't let the Lord rescue you yet. Perhaps you think you have to clean yourself up first or that He wouldn't want you. Hear me say this: these are lies! God wants you. Now and as you are. You can't clean yourself up enough to be perfect—that's the whole point. Only He can clean you. He just wants you to admit you can't do it yourself and you need Him. He wants you to let go and loosen that tight fist around your life and surrender it to Him. Will you? Right now?

Or perhaps you think you've been rescued because you've gone to church your whole life or are a good person (although hopefully the lying and stealing we just talked about shakes you up a bit). Maybe what you're really doing is trusting in your own righteousness—or to use a less Christian-y word, your good-person-ness. Going to church and being a good person won't save you.

Answer this: If you died tonight and God said, "Why should I let you into heaven?" what would you say? If you said something about how you're not that bad or you're a good person, then you're putting your trust in yourself rather than in what Jesus did for you on the cross. If you answered with something like, "Well, I'm not perfect, but can't God overlook that because He's so loving?" then your view of God's holiness is way too small. God will not allow anyone who is less than perfect to dwell in His presence in heaven forever. That is why He chose excruciating death and glorious resurrection—because sin is a big deal.

Scotty Smith says it this way:

> Failure to love God as he deserves and demands is the essence of what the Bible calls sin.… Certainly, as Creator, God has every right to expect his creation to comply with his design and intent. For God *not* to judge and punish sin would be a miscarriage of justice and a contradiction of his essential being. In our own court systems we impeach judges who do not uphold the law and administer justice.… This is the heart of the good news, the gospel. Jesus has been punished for our sins so that the floodgate of God's affection can be loosed on us like a healing river![4]

God has given you an incredible rescue story … or stands waiting to.

"Let the redeemed of the LORD tell their story—those he redeemed from the hand of the foe" (Ps. 107:2).

## God Redeems

God not only rescues but also redeems. Redemption holds the element of deliverance not only *from* something but also *to* something: from slavery to freedom. God scoops us up, takes all our broken pieces, and turns them into something beautiful.

But redemption presupposes there is something bad that needs to be redeemed. Perhaps it's something done to you or something you've done. God uses even your mistakes and masterfully makes them beautiful.

He takes our sin
head-on and transforms
it into a megaphone
for His fame.

Your mistakes don't make you unusable. In fact, there is no place for shame if you are a follower of Jesus. If you have submitted your life to Him, you have been declared innocent. Your guilt was transferred to Christ the moment you admitted that He was God and that you had sinned against Him.

You are not defined by your sin; you are defined by Jesus' blood. Satan wants to accuse you and tell you that you are less than. But God says you are holy (Eph. 4:24), the light of the world (Matt. 5:14), a co-heir with Christ sharing His inheritance (Rom. 8:17), a new creation (2 Cor. 5:17), a saint (1 Cor. 1:2; Eph. 1:1; Phil. 1:1; Col. 1:2 ESV), God's workmanship (Eph. 2:10 ESV), blameless (Phil. 2:15), chosen (Col. 3:12), adopted (Rom. 8:15), deeply, radically, and unconditionally loved (Col. 3:12), and being used for His purposes (Rom. 8:28).

Your new identity came not because you earned it and not because you deserve it, but because He rescued and redeemed you. No matter how much Satan or your old self wants to make you feel shame, the reality is that you have been declared forgiven, innocent.

There is no condemnation for those in Christ (see Rom. 8:1). After all, Jesus Himself is a descendant of Rahab, a prostitute, and Bathsheba, an adulteress. God redeems at the expense of His own hurt. He takes our sin head-on and transforms it into a megaphone for His fame. Therefore, He is worthy of your full confidence. Others will fail you and you will fail too, but God never fails. His plans always succeed. No one—not even you yourself—can so mess up what God wants to do that it's beyond redemption. When others fail you or when you totally mess up, put your hope in the Redeemer and know that you are not beyond His reach.

Have you ever wondered why God let the greatest deceiver of all time be in the same location as the most naive people of all time? Why did God allow the serpent into the garden of Eden? Does that not seem like a recipe for disaster? Well, He did, and it went poorly. The deceiver tricked Adam and Eve into disobeying God, ultimately breaking not only the whole of mankind but also our planet. You and I have never messed up *that* big.

All sin can be traced back to that minute. And yet, we don't see God having a meltdown because His good design got warped. He hates sin, but He saw past it to redemption. God saw this coming. He knew that His character of being a rescuer and redeemer would be revealed through it, and He valued His glory above the pain marked by sin. And ultimately, seeing His glory and character is the best thing for us.

I tend to value perfection over redemption (and maybe you do too). Let me explain. Earlier, I shared about adopting our boys. After adopting, we got pregnant … four times! The first time, I got ignorant comments quite often. They didn't bother me that much, since God has made me a pretty gracious person. But if my boys were to hear them, that would be a whole different story.

For instance, one day when I told someone I was pregnant, the person said, "Bet you wish you would have waited." I was in absolute shock, trying to figure out what else the person could mean besides thinking I wouldn't have wanted my boys. The next day, as I told someone else about my pregnancy, the person next to her excitedly said "with her *own*," as if my boys aren't my own! If my boys had heard either of those comments, how would their young minds have understood that these people were just speaking a bit ignorantly? They wouldn't have been able to, and that is how lies get set in a heart.

What if they'd heard the comment, "So which boy is the 'real' son?" Words like this made me want to control everything my children ever heard. I thought, *I have to be with them every second so I can help them recognize these stupid comments as lies.* But the reality is that I cannot be with them every second. I have to trust God with them.

God doesn't do things my way. If I had my way, everything would be perfect. There would be no pain or suffering, and no one would believe any lies. But He allows awful things because they give Him the opportunity to show Himself as the great Redeemer. So, the chances are that my boys *will* believe lies, and the chances are that I won't know what they are. But hope says that God knows and is using those lies for something greater. He will allow hard things, and He will redeem them, and then even I will say it was worth it. Redemption is beautiful but comes from pain.

You are unshaken
because God will
redeem whatever
comes your way.

God doesn't seem to think that sparing us from pain is as great an idea as we do. It seems He sees the beauty that can be found only on the other side of pain. God seems to value redemption over perfection. Perhaps that's because our deficiencies trigger His redemption. Our failures spotlight His grace. Maybe you or someone close to you hasn't seen God's redemption yet, and all you see is pain, lack, and failure. It's like one of my favorite songs by Danny Gokey, "Haven't Seen It Yet":

> *Have you been praying and you still have no answers?…*
> *It's like the brightest sunrise*
> *Waiting on the other side of the darkest night*
> *Don't ever lose hope, hold on and believe*
> *Maybe you just haven't seen it, just haven't seen it yet.*[5]

Maybe you just haven't seen it yet and your sunrise is about to burst forth. Put your hope in God, the One who redeems. You are unshaken because God will redeem whatever comes your way.

## God Restores

My friend Amy had the worst day of her life on July 6, 2010. She was giving her kids a bath. She took her little two-year-old son, Gore, out of the tub and put his pajama shirt and diaper on. She went to grab his pajama pants, and when she returned, he was gone.

She became frantic. How could a little boy go missing in just a moment?

After twenty-five minutes of searching, she ran toward an irrigation ditch and heard screams. She saw her cousin walking toward her with her little son in his arms. Gore was white and lifeless in his pajama shirt and diaper. They had found him submerged under a log in the fast-moving water of the irrigation ditch.

She thought he was dead, but they took him to the hospital anyway, where the doctors said he had a 1 percent chance of survival. They feared that even if they managed to restart his heart, Gore had suffered irreparable brain damage.

After an hour, they restarted his heart and did therapeutic hypothermia, an experimental treatment in which the body temperature is lowered—in Gore's case, to ninety degrees—in order to protect the brain and allow healing.

While doctors slowly warmed Gore back up to normal body temperature, they all watched for purposeful movement, any sign of brain activity. Suddenly, Gore started moving, and he opened his eyes. He used the signal his parents had taught him to tell them he was hungry.

An MRI scan of Gore's brain came back with astonishing results: perfectly normal. A few days later, Gore walked out of the hospital on his own. The doctors couldn't fully explain how this little boy had come back to life, much less with no brain damage, after being underwater and without a heartbeat for so long.

Amy tells the whole miraculous story in her book, *Giving Up Gore*.[6] It's a tearjerker in the most redeeming ways.

Amy's story is a reminder that God is the same today, yesterday, and forever. His power has not diminished since raising Lazarus from the dead, and neither have any of His other incredible attributes. We serve a God who restores life. In fact, He does it every single day, many times a day. We can't see beyond death, so our sight is quite limited. But there is no separation of time between death and life for Him. When we look at death, we see only someone who died, but He sees a person to whom He gave eternal life.

God restores not only our broken bodies but also our broken relationships. Remember the prostitute from Luke 7 (in chapter 2) whom Jesus bragged about after she'd wiped His feet with her hair? That is a beautiful picture of how Jesus restores people to their communities.

From the moment Jesus entered Simon's house, Simon did not give Him a basin to wash His feet, and he did not greet Him with a kiss. What Simon did was offensive. I

We tend to think
in terms of now,
but God's plans
are bigger than
the right now.

wonder if he was slightly jealous of Jesus and that might be why he went out of his way to prove that Jesus was nothing special.

Perhaps this is why the prostitute was crying. Was she wondering, *Don't they know who He is? Why are they treating Him this way?* So she began to anoint His feet with her most precious item, the oil from her alabaster jar, and to wipe them with her hair, maybe to make up for Simon's rudeness. Simon was so consumed with exposing her sin that he was blind to his own.

I love how Jesus doesn't just sweep things under the carpet but addresses attitudes and actions. He brought Simon's offenses to his attention, and He exposed the lies Simon was believing about the woman. At this point, a humble man would have apologized for his lack of respect and thanked the woman for compensating for him. But Simon was not able to recognize his faults. All he could do was point the finger at the outwardly "sinful" woman.

Still talking to Simon, Jesus turned to the woman. How beautiful! Looking right into her eyes, He started bragging on her in front of the entire room of people. Who, in these men's eyes, would be the most undeserving of His honor? A prostitute. But Jesus seized the opportunity to brag on her because of her faith.

This action would have been shocking to the men in that room. Not only did Jesus praise and honor a despised woman, but He also made her the noble hero. And by giving her public honor, He restored her to community.

We have hope because Jesus will restore all things. We tend to think in terms of now, but God's plans are bigger than the right now. He *will* heal, but that doesn't mean it will be now or even this side of eternity. We see so dimly. He *will* make all things new. We *will* get bodies that won't decay, and all things *will* be restored.

You are not hopeless. You have been rescued and will be fully restored, and the years the locusts have eaten will be fully redeemed (see Joel 2:25). You have a future filled with hope.

# CONNECT WITH THE LORD

Watch the chapter 3 video now. Find the video using the QR code or link on page 22.

## God Rescues, Redeems, and Restores You

• How have you seen God rescue you?

• What are some ways you have seen God take failure or something evil or painful and make it beautiful?

• What are some recent times you have failed yourself or someone else has failed you? What promise of God can you cling to in those situations?

• In what areas of your life are you still waiting to see God's redemption unfold?

• How have you felt beyond redemption?

• What do you tend to turn to when you are in distress? Give an example.

• Look up the following passages, and write down how they describe God and what He has done:

    Deuteronomy 9:26

    2 Samuel 7:23–24

Psalm 34:22

Isaiah 43:1–3

Isaiah 54:5

Ephesians 1:7–8

Colossians 1:13–14

1 Peter 1:18–21

- In the following categories, ask God to remind you of ways He has rescued and redeemed things in your life:

Relationships

Circumstances

Addictions

Lies

Failures

Our actions and emotions often reveal what we really believe about God, ourselves, and others.

## Truth Chart

| | |
|---|---|
| • 1. What have you been discouraged about recently? | • 6. What is one way you can act on what is true? |
| • 2. How is it impacting your life: feelings, thoughts, choices? | • 5. If you believed God *forgave you*, how would it impact your wants and actions? |
| • 3. What does it show that you believe about God? | • 4. If you truly believed God *rescues and redeems*, how would it impact your feelings? |

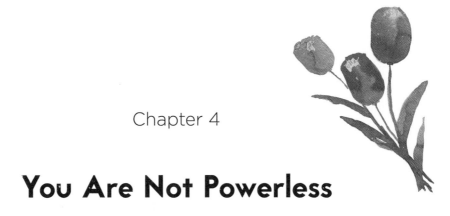

Chapter 4

# You Are Not Powerless

A feeling many women share is that we are not enough, that we don't and won't have enough, and that we are powerless to do anything about it.

In response, the world shouts shallow sound bites and superficial fixes at us, like this one: "Don't ever say you're not good enough, because if that person can't see how amazing you are, then that person is the one who's not good enough."[1]

It's a mantra we hear often. It's a banner of self-love, self-acceptance, and self-sufficiency. There's just one problem: we *aren't* enough. That's actually the point. We need Jesus, His grace, His love, and His enablement each moment. We cannot do this life on our own.

So does that mean we are powerless? No! It means our brokenness and weakness are where we find His grace sufficient. "But he said to me, 'My grace is sufficient for you, for my power is made perfect in weakness.' Therefore I will boast all the more gladly about my weaknesses, so that Christ's power may rest on me" (2 Cor. 12:9). You have the power and the ability because of the Holy Spirit working inside you to do what God has called you to do. Though we are not enough, Jesus is, and *He* is our sufficiency (see 2 Cor. 3:5).

It's not fun to admit we are not enough. Yet admitting our weakness, our dependency, allows us to stop putting so much energy into trying to look and feel like we

We don't need to keep hearing how we are good enough; we need to be reminded that Jesus is good enough for us.

have it all together. Acknowledging that we are not enough allows us to be honest and vulnerable, and it also makes space for others to show up with their faults and weaknesses.

Please don't buy into the lie that you are enough. It will actually lead to more disappointment, more self-doubt, and more frustration with yourself and the world around you. You are not enough—but your mighty, wonder-working God is enough for you! And He has intimately crafted you to reveal His character in a way no one else can.

But just because you're not enough in your own self-sufficiency doesn't mean you're not immensely valuable and deeply loved. It doesn't mean you're powerless. On the contrary, it means that the very same power that raised Jesus from the dead is alive in you. Being not enough just means you can't exist in a vacuum. You were created to need the God who loves and values you.

The beauty of lacking the power to do it all on your own is that it makes room for Jesus' sufficiency to be seen through you—and that is more than "enough." We don't need to keep hearing how *we* are good enough; we need to be reminded that Jesus is good enough for us. You may be weak, but His power is strong in you. You may be lacking, but God is your strength. He is enough, He is able, and He will sustain you.

> But we have this treasure in jars of clay to show that this all-surpassing power is from God and not from us. We are hard pressed on every side, but not crushed; perplexed, but not in despair; persecuted, but not abandoned; struck down, but not destroyed. (2 Cor. 4:7–9)

## God Is Enough

I love taking family photos. And in them, I love to have coordinating outfits and a beautiful background. But when our kids were younger, they didn't cooperate very well.

One time, when our oldest was around four and the others were three and one, I dragged Austin to a photo shoot, doing my best to convince him that our kids were going to do great. They were older than they were at our last attempt, and I was sure they would do much better than the other time we'd had a photo shoot. After all, the pictures were going to be cherished forever.

Well, Uriah was a grump most of the time, and Asher was over-the-top out of control. We ended up leaving because Asher fell and was dripping blood everywhere. Not great for pictures, really. Yeah, Austin was right: it didn't go so great.

Why is it we long for that perfect shot? Why don't we want to enlarge a picture of "crazy" to mount on the wall? I think it's because our culture values perfection and looking our best. When was the last time you encouraged someone to try just a little, give just enough, or order the second-best thing on the menu?

If our goal in life is to have it all together (and to expect others to be perfect as well), then we don't point people to Jesus and His sufficiency but rather to our own sufficiency or lack of it. God's perfection is enough to satisfy our insufficiencies. Why not delight in that? Why not be vulnerable and let our flaws spotlight His greatness?

When Austin and I were planning our wedding, I couldn't think of just the right song for our first dance. I simply picked a song, but months later, I heard the perfect song and was so sad I hadn't thought of it in time. In my discouragement, the Lord reminded me that Jesus died for my failures too. Our failures shine a spotlight on God's grace.

Have you ever heard of wabi-sabi? It's the Japanese art of finding beauty in imperfection. We often see it as pottery that has been broken and then reconstructed with gold in the cracks. Sometimes, the Japanese would clean up their backyard sand and, just before they were done, shake the leaves from a tree enough to create a little mess; they did this as a reminder to embrace imperfection, a sign of beauty.

Embracing imperfection for imperfection's sake is crazy and definitely not beautiful. But embracing imperfection to display Jesus as the Perfect One … now that's an idea! That sort of mindset reminds us that we don't have it all together, because Jesus is our togetherness. And really, don't we all need the constant reminder to keep looking to Jesus' sufficiency instead of our own?

Because of the gospel, we have been stamped with a new identity that is not based on anything we've done but rather upon something freely given to us because of what Jesus did. And this new identity defines every aspect of our lives. He declared us forgiven, righteous, adopted, accepted, free, and co-heirs with Christ. No longer do our sins, failures, or weaknesses define us.

The gospel gives us a new way to live with and relate to others that isn't based on us (or them) being good enough. However, it's so easy to stop leaning into Jesus' sufficiency, either out of condemnation or pride. Both keep us from experiencing and displaying to others the God who is enough.

Apart from Christ, as I have said, we are not enough. But neither is any other person. People will never be enough for us. They will never measure up to our standards, hopes, and dreams. They will always fall short because, just like us, they have this crazy disease called sin. Another person will never be able to fulfill our deepest longings. Only God can. And there is so much freedom in releasing people from being our source of life. Rather than looking to ourselves or others to be enough, we need to continually set our gaze on Christ, the all-sufficient One.

This reminds me of a story of a boy who wanted to see Jesus (see John 6:1–13). Perhaps he had been among the crowd that had seen Jesus perform miracles so he wanted to be around Him more. He learned that Jesus had gone to the other side of the lake. Perhaps he begged and begged his mom to go with him, but Mom had too many other obligations. Finally, she gave in and let him go. We don't know why. Maybe a relative decided to go along with him. But we do know she packed him a mighty big lunch for just a boy: five loaves of bread and two fish.

I don't know about you, but when I pack a lunch for my kiddo, I am not packing for the others who will be along. I probably would have packed a couple slices of bread with a little bit of tuna fish in between. So I like this mama. She seems to have been pretty thoughtful and generous. Perhaps she wondered and worried if even that large amount would be enough. Little did she know that her thoughtfulness and her son's faith would be rewarded by his getting to see Jesus revealed as the bread of life.

Mom's generosity must have rubbed off on her boy, because he gave all he had to Jesus to do with as He pleased. He didn't have enough to feed everyone, but Jesus stepped in and used what he had and made it enough. That's the kind of work God does: making enough from the not-enough.

I've shared with you that Austin and I were unable to have kids and how God first gave us our two boys through adoption. We still wanted more kids, and we heard about something called "snowflake adoption." It is adopting an embryo that was made through in-vitro fertilization. There are more than four hundred thousand yet-to-be-born babies in freezers waiting to be adopted, and as of this writing, only two hundred people had adopted any.

We were moved to adopt some of these frozen babies, and we saw God leading us through verses like Galatians 6:10: "As we have opportunity, let us do good to all people." We believed God had given us "opportunity" to provide a womb for a baby to grow in. We believed the right thing for us to do was to adopt an embryo that had been left frozen.

So we started the process. But after three doctor's appointments, each worse than the one before, things came into perspective. The process was going to be twice as much money as we thought, the drive to the doctor was super far, and I was going to have to give myself shots (I *hate* needles) every day for three months! And the list went on and on.

On my drive home from the first doctor, I was crying and telling God I wasn't sure I could do it. He reminded me that *life* was worth the inconvenience. So I determined not to bow to the idol of convenience.

After doctor's appointment number two, where I heard about the one-and-a-half-inch-long needle I would have to inject into myself every day—in addition to having to swear off coffee, be on bed rest for two days, and refrain from lifting my boys for two weeks—I doubted even more. I thought, *God, for real, I really don't think I can do this.*

And finally, after doctor's appointment number three, in which some tests didn't work and the doctors talked about doing some even more invasive procedures, I started questioning if God really wanted us to do this.

Austin describes it as our faith bumping up against our flesh, and whenever that happens, we tend to look for a lifeline. After all this, we began to question our "calling" to move forward in this adoption. Once it got hard, we started looking to our feelings or circumstances to figure out whether or not God wanted us to move forward. What we should've done was read His Word and remember that if He for real wants us to do something, then it's something He wants us to do whether we feel like it or not.

But once again God showed His grace to be sufficient. The day after the third appointment, He led me to verse after verse that opened my eyes and gave me strength to trust Him and His Word more than my feelings. His Word enabled me to walk by faith through the inconvenient.

Here are the verses He spoke to me regarding moving forward with this adoption:

- But rejoice inasmuch as you participate in the sufferings of Christ, so that you may be overjoyed when his glory is revealed. (1 Pet. 4:13)
- Let us not become weary in doing good. (Gal. 6:9)
- Therefore, I urge you, brothers and sisters, in view of God's mercy, to offer your bodies as a living sacrifice, holy and pleasing to God—this is your true and proper worship. (Rom. 12:1)
- I consider that our present sufferings are not worth comparing with the glory that will be revealed in us. (Rom. 8:18)
- Whatever you did for one of the least of these brothers and sisters of mine, you did for me. (Matt. 25:40)
- For I have the desire to do what is good, but I cannot carry it out.… Who will rescue me from this body that is subject to death? Thanks be to God, who delivers me through Jesus Christ our Lord! (Rom. 7:18, 24–25)

- You see, at just the right time, when we were still powerless, Christ died for the ungodly. (Rom. 5:6)

    Jesus took on physical affliction for the benefit of those who couldn't do anything about their condition. Through His suffering, He freed us from what held us back from doing what we were created to do—glorify Him. Carrying this baby would give it life and thus the opportunity to do what he or she was created to do—glorify God.

- But he said to me, "My grace is sufficient for you, for my power is made perfect in weakness." Therefore I will boast all the more gladly about my weaknesses, so that Christ's power may rest on me. (2 Cor. 12:9)

We made the decision to move forward, and soon we went in for the trial transfer. This was the invasive procedure where the medical staff would see if it was possible to place real embryos in my womb. Everything looked good.

But a few weeks later, in a matter of a couple of days, some wild things happened. Austin got a phone call from the adoption agency; they had lost our fingerprints, and we would need to start over. While he was on the phone, I got a call from the embryo adoption agency; the woman told us that the embryos we were going to adopt had been placed with someone else. As Austin and I both hung up, we were in shock. What was God doing?

The next day, I missed my period. The day after that, I took a pregnancy test, and it came back positive. The woman who had been told she couldn't have kids was pregnant! Nine months later, I gave birth to a little girl. We named her Eden, which means "delight"—and she is!

It's still a mystery why God had me go through the emotional process of being willing to offer up the use of my body for the life of another, but I believe God used that trial transfer to do something inside my body, something that made me able to have kids. After all, it was the next month we got pregnant after seven years of being infertile.

God often doesn't give us the big picture. We can see only a step at a time, and it isn't until we look back that we can see more. His grace is like that. He gives us what we need each step of the way: perspective, hope, vision, strength, motivation, and so much more. He takes us by the right hand and says, "This is the way; walk in it" (Isa. 30:21). Our vision isn't good enough to see the big picture. We don't have the ability to see the future, but He does.

The Lord is enough, and in Him we have all we need. There has never been and never will be a time when God will not be enough for you.

## God Enables

My friend Abigail was driving home from Costco during rush hour and passed a pregnant girl who was asking for gas on the street corner. Abigail was halfway home, but the Holy Spirit clearly impressed on her to turn around and help. So she did a quick U-turn.

As she filled the girl's car with gas, Abigail asked about her situation and support system. She got her number so she could offer tangible help if possible. Over the course of the next month, they established a relationship. The girl had nothing for the baby, so Abigail gave her all her daughter's old clothes and baby accessories.

Not long after, Abigail got a call from the girl. She was in the hospital. The police had been called by people who were concerned about a very pregnant woman standing on the corner asking for help. It turned out she had undiagnosed preeclampsia, and she had been taken to the hospital, where she had delivered the baby that night via C-section. She had called Abigail to ask if she wanted to meet the baby. Abigail went to the hospital and got to meet not only the baby but also the birth dad, who was almost thirty years older than the new mom.

During her hospital stay, Child and Family Services (CFS) was contacted, so she was under constant surveillance at the hospital. Ultimately, CFS determined that the baby girl could not go home with Mom but would be allowed to go with Grandpa, Mom's dad. That had been Abigail's worst fear, because from the beginning she'd seen serious red flags about him and had prayed constantly that he wouldn't get guardianship. She later learned that CFS had removed Mom from her parents when she was an adolescent.

Later, the young mom called Abigail again from the hospital, asking if she had a car seat. Earlier that day, the Holy Spirit had unmistakably told Abigail to buy a car seat. She had immediately gotten on Craigslist. The very first item listed was a car seat for twenty dollars. She contacted the seller and agreed to meet after she got off work at 5:00 p.m. The young mom was very upset by the delay, because it meant she would have to wait a few more hours at the hospital, and she just wanted her dad to be able to take the baby home.

Abigail later learned that during those few hours of waiting, the supervising CFS worker had done more research on Grandpa. What she found horrified her, so she had immediately called the hospital and instructed them not to let Grandpa leave with the baby at any cost. So that few-hour gap had saved the baby from going to the same home situation that her mom had been raised in, and removed from, on a Native American reservation.

That same day, Abigail took her two-year-old daughter to her swim lesson. While she was there, an older lady recognized her: "Oh, you're the friend of the girl who just had a baby! I'm a labor and delivery nurse."

Abigail told her the situation and said she had offered to help the young mom with the baby. The nurse said she wished Abigail had let them know that while the mom and baby had been at the hospital, because that would've helped them make decisions. Abigail called her husband, who worked at the hospital and knew the CFS director, and had him relay that he and Abigail were willing to help.

CFS gave them emergency guardianship because of Abigail's prior relationship with the mom. With only a two-hour warning, my friend Abigail and her husband were getting a newborn baby to care for. They had nothing for a baby because Abigail had just given everything they had to the birth mom. But their community jumped in, and by the end of the night, their nine-foot-long dining table was piled high with baby accessories and supplies.

The CFS agent brought the baby girl from the hospital to Abigail and her husband and began going over the emergency guardianship paperwork. "Uh-oh," she said, "Mom is Native American, which means this is under the Indian Child Welfare Act. I'm afraid this baby is going to have to be placed with a Native family."

But the things that surprise us are no surprise to God. Without missing a beat, Abigail said, "Well, I'm an enrolled tribal member. Does that help?"

Shocked, the CFS agent said, "Yes! Because that makes this an Indian household!"

When they later went through foster care training, they learned what a huge deal Abigail's enrollment actually was. If Abigail had not been an enrolled tribal member, the baby would have been transferred within days.

This was the beginning of a whirlwind journey that only God could have orchestrated. They conducted visits with the birth mom for a few months, until she was picked up by police and incarcerated for felony charges. After over two years in jail, she was given a long-term sentence and transferred to prison. After two-and-a-half years of constant ups and downs, my friend Abigail and her family were able to officially adopt the baby girl.

God uses any of His children who are available to Him to accomplish His great purposes—even in deeply broken situations.

We can see only dimly, as in an imperfect mirror (see 1 Cor. 13:12). We can see only a little of the big picture. Let me show you what I mean. You've probably heard the famous story of David and Goliath (see 1 Sam. 17). You've probably thought of Goliath as the big bad guy and David as the underdog. But we can't see what God sees, and we don't know what God knows. Let me give you a bit of background on these guys.

Goliath was huge: six cubits and a span, likely nine feet six inches tall. He was the Philistines' champion, the one they put onto the battlefield to scare the Israelites. And it worked. The Israelite army was terrified.

But now with modern medical understanding, we know that people who grow to be this large have a rare genetic disorder. Goliath, his brother, and three sons, who were also giants, likely had a hereditary autosomal dominant pituitary gene.[2] Basically, this is a pituitary gland dysfunction. A tumor grows and presses on the pituitary gland, causing the person to never stop growing.[3]

Besides Goliath's size, some other clues in Scripture lead us to believe he may have had this disorder. A tumor pressing on the pituitary gland may also press on the optic nerve, affecting eyesight. In 1 Samuel 17, we hear Goliath mock David with his "sticks" (v. 43). But David carried one stick, not many.

We also find that Goliath was led to the battlefield by an armor-bearer. Was this a military procession, or did someone have to go in front of Goliath because he couldn't see well? In those days, armor-bearers were not uncommon, but David didn't get one. Typically, these would be the guys who carry weapons, kind of like a caddy in golf—not someone who would go in front of a mighty warrior to lead him. It could be that Goliath had poor eyesight and the Israelites had no idea.[4]

Now let's take a closer look at David. David was the youngest of a bunch of brothers. I don't know about you, but from what I've seen, the youngest kid from a family with a lot of older brothers tends to be pretty tough. He was a shepherd who hung out in fields with the sheep, watching for wolves, even as a boy. I'm not sure I would be brave enough to let my little boy fend off wolves. Heck, I'm not even sure *I* would be brave enough to face wolves. But that was David's training ground.

Out in the desert, he practiced with his sling and rocks. What else is there to do all day but practice? So the kid got good. Really good, and really brave. He ended up killing a lion and a bear, for goodness' sake (see v. 36). We have mountain lions where I live, and they are absolutely terrifying. If I got in a fight with a mountain lion, the lion would win.

Now let's consider David's slingshot. In ancient times, the military had groups known as slingers. Their weapon was the slingshot. Slingers got so good with this weapon that they could fire rocks at the velocity of a speeding bullet.[5] David was a slinger. God had been training him for this moment since he was a boy.

Let's think about the fight. A disabled giant with bad eyesight went up against a skilled slinger with a weapon as deadly as a gun. David outwardly seemed like the underdog, and yet God had prepared him for such a time as this. God had been giving him the ability he would need to handle this exact situation. God had enabled him. The Israelites had no way of knowing what we suspect today about Goliath and no way of knowing how God had prepared David. David didn't even know his advantage over Goliath, but he knew God was with him. He ran to the battlefield trusting that God would enable him.

God is able, and He enables us to do what we and others may see as impossible.

Some might get upset with me here, thinking my version of this story causes it to lose its power. But to me, it makes it all the more powerful. It lets us see how present and active God is in our lives. It lets us see how He is preparing and providing for us, giving us what we need to walk by faith in what He has called us to do. We can't and won't be able to see all the details, but God can. When He calls you to step out in faith and trust Him, it's because He sees the whole picture. You see something big and scary, but He sees how He's already trained and prepared you and set the table strategically for you. He will come through for you.

One of my favorite parts of this story is David's motivation. He didn't run to the battle because he thought *he* was so great but because he knew God was. His eyes were not on his own ability and self-sufficiency but on God's. His confidence was more in God's ability than in his own, and nothing deterred him from that perspective.

Before the fight, David had just brought bread and cheese to his brothers, at their father's request. When he arrived, he left his things with the keeper of supplies and ran to the battle lines. When he got there, Goliath came out, and David saw all the soldiers run off scared. So David started asking about the reward for killing Goliath. Here is what his brother Eliab said to him: "Why have you come down here? And with whom did you leave those few sheep in the wilderness? I know how conceited you are and how wicked your heart is" (v. 28).

Ouch! Doesn't that make you sick to your stomach? How belittling and crushing to have someone talk about how worthless your little job is and then assume your motives are evil. It is humiliating and painful. It makes me so proud of David that he responded with a simple, "What have I done now?" (v. 29 HCSB). Can you sense the sarcasm? A simple yet powerful question.

Good for him, standing up to his bully of a brother but not resorting to name calling. And he didn't fall into self-pity and give up, either. He kept asking about Goliath and the reward for killing him. Even in this, the Lord was instilling determination in him. He'd need it later in life because God was going to have him walk through some pretty tough situations as king. Truly, God uses all things for the good of those who love Him (see Rom. 8:28).

All these amazing stories of God showing off by empowering His people reveal a God who enables His people. Abigail, my friend, and David, the future king, are ordinary people that God used for extraordinary purposes. Not because they were so great, but because God is. God enabled people who were submitted to Him to do things beyond their own comprehension.

God can train and is training you even now, and He will give you what you need when you need it. "And God is able to bless you abundantly, so that in all things at all times, having all that you need, you will abound in every good work" (2 Cor. 9:8). But if Abigail hadn't turned around at that first prompting, or if David hadn't been content to be a shepherd, giving him time to learn to sling, they wouldn't have gotten to see God's power work through them.

Keep walking by faith, taking the next step, and be patient, because you won't be shaken.

# God Sustains

While I was pregnant with Malachi, my fourth kiddo (second biological), I developed anxiety. I had never experienced anything like it, and before experiencing it myself, I couldn't really understand what people meant when they talked about it. I figured they should just stop worrying and believe what God says. How gracious of God to let me experience it to keep me from hurting people with my counsel.

In case you've never experienced anxiety, the best way to describe it is that your body has an intense feeling of fear and your mind is trying to figure out why, so it attaches to any little worry and exaggerates it.

I remember a day during this pregnancy when I looked in the mirror and wondered how I was going to get through life like this. I couldn't even imagine getting through the day. Before going in to have a C-section, I was literally unable to stop shaking, terrified I was going to die and not be there for my kids.

The delivery went fine, but the anxiety continued … day after day, until I stopped breastfeeding, and then it abruptly went away. But before I stopped, I had come to believe that God was going to have me live with that anxiety for the rest of my life. I figured that because I had an ailment that day, I was going to have it all my days. But that's not what happened. Once the anxiety stopped, I could look back and see that God had sustained me through each day.

Throughout Scripture, God is described as the One who sustains all things. God sustains His children through difficult times: "Surely God is my help; the Lord is the one who sustains me" (Ps. 54:4). Our strength will eventually fail, but His will not. Nothing that has been created can sustain itself. Only the Creator, the One who holds all things together, can. He has unending strength.

Jesus taught us to pray, "Give us today our daily bread" (Matt. 6:11). Just as He provided food for the Israelites each day in the wilderness, God meets our needs each day—in a slow, bit-by-bit way. It's like the perfectly timed nugget my friend Christina told me after

The Lord left this
thorn to give Paul
sustaining strength.

I'd had Eden (my third child but my first biologically). When I wondered how I was going to make it to the post office with two small runners and a baby, she said, "God's grace is sufficient when you need it, not before." It's similar to the widow with the oil (see 1 Kings 17:8–16). The oil miraculously lasted as long as she needed it. This is God's sustaining power. God gives us what we need when we need it, and usually not before.

We can also see the sustaining character of God in creation. What He created reveals His invisible attributes, divine nature, and eternal power (see Rom. 1:20). Consider what bears show us about God's character. Bears nurse their cubs for five months, yet they don't drink a drop of water during that time. Not one drop. How in the world is that possible? Their fat breaks down into water, and they have little internal factories that turn their urine into proteins to nourish the body while feeding the cub.

Another interesting thing about bears is that they lose only 20 percent of their strength during five months of hibernation. If we were to lie down for five months, we would lose 90 percent of our strength. Ninety percent! So how does this happen? How are they immune to the "use it or lose it" principle? Well, during hibernation, bears go into violent chills and tense up, which causes them to keep their muscle strength. This is very important, since they will need to be strong enough to gather food or possibly fight after waking from hibernation.

Bears show us that God knows how to sustain us even when it seems impossible. He knows exactly what we need to walk out the good plan He has for us. Surely, if the Lord built the bear to be sustained without a drop of water while nursing and to retain muscle strength during hibernation, He can sustain us through thick and thin.

The Lord will allow times when He will wait to rescue us and will instead sustain us through something painful. This is what He did with Paul:

> Three times I pleaded with the Lord to take it away from me. But he said to me, "My grace is sufficient for you, for my power is made perfect in weakness." Therefore I will boast all the more gladly about my weaknesses, so that Christ's power may rest on me. (2 Cor. 12:8–9)

There was something in Paul's life that he wanted the Lord to remove, but God said no. He didn't take Paul's problem away but rather used it to keep Paul dependent on Him. The Lord left this thorn to give Paul sustaining strength.

As He did with Paul, God will allow pain in your life … but He will sustain you through it. He is and has all you need, and He will never fail to provide for you as you step out and walk by faith.

Sometimes, it feels as if the whole world will fall apart if we don't control it and hold onto it with a tight fist. And yet this very attitude leads to a sense of constantly feeling out of control. God is the One who holds all things together (see Col. 1:17). Let this settle your soul: everything you see, feel, touch, and experience is being held together by Jesus. What security and hope that offers you! Knowing that, you can live unshaken.

"The Son is the radiance of God's glory and the exact representation of his being, sustaining all things by his powerful word. After he had provided purification for sins, he sat down at the right hand of the Majesty in heaven" (Heb. 1:3).

# CONNECT WITH THE LORD

Watch the chapter 4 video now. Find the video using the QR code or link on page 22.

## God Is Enough; He Enables and Sustains You

• Describe a time when you felt powerless.

• Describe a time when you saw God sustain someone.

• How do these passages show us that God is enough?

Psalm 46:1

Luke 1:37

John 16:33

Romans 8:31–39

2 Corinthians 12:9

Ephesians 3:20

Philippians 4:19

## Truth Chart

| | |
|---|---|
| • 1. In what ways have you recently felt "not enough"? | • 6. What is one way you can act on what is true? |
| • 2. How is it impacting your life: feelings, thoughts, choices? | • 5. If you believed God could and would *enable you*, how would it impact your wants and actions? |
| • 3. What does it show that you believe about God? | • 4. If you believed God was *enough for you*, how would it impact your feelings? |

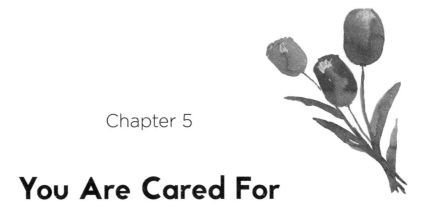

## Chapter 5

# You Are Cared For

When I was in college, I got a parking ticket that was somewhat unjustified. My sweet friend Christina, who has a passion for justice, took my ticket and marched herself right into the campus police office to plead my case. She took on my problem and freely gave her time and energy to stand up for me. And thanks to Christina, the campus police cleared my ticket. What a picture of Jesus, the One who pleads our case.

When Christina stepped in on my behalf, I felt deeply loved and cared for. I feel cared for when my husband steps in to help me out of dumb mistakes, or when a friend shoots me an encouraging text, or when my kids rub my feet. What makes you feel cared for?

We all long to feel cared for. From the moment we are born, we have an obvious need to be cared for—and at the end of our lives, our need to be cared for is again obvious. It may not be as obvious in the middle years, but it's still true. People require care.

The person with an independent streak may say, "I don't need anyone," but that couldn't be further from the truth. Just as our cells need energy and our lungs need oxygen, our emotions need connection for well-being. We all need to be taken care of, and it's nothing to be ashamed of. And though we are all made to have Christinas in our lives, ultimately, that care is fully found only in the Lord. He is our provider and the source of everything we will ever need. People will fail in how they care for us, but God never will.

When someone cares for us, trust is built, and a sense of security develops. But people just can't care for us perfectly. They will always fail to care for us in the ways we hope for or even need. They can never be our ultimate providers.

But God can't fail. He is precise and exact, and He does not make mistakes. He is 100 percent worthy of your full trust. He will never fail in how He cares for you. Let that sink in. He will never be less than perfect in how He cares for you. He will come through for you; He will fight for you and lead you into the truth.

## God Will Come Through for You

I first met Austin after I returned from a six-month missionary training program that ended with a mission trip to Nepal. While I was away, most of my friends graduated and moved on, so I was looking to meet some new friends.

I went to a barbecue, and a nice guy brought me a hamburger. I was so impressed with his thoughtfulness. I thought, *Wow, I wonder if we're going to be friends.*

The very next day, I was invited to yet another barbecue (apparently, that was the thing to do that summer in Durango). I had just gotten to the house when a young man rode up on his ten-speed bike in his Pizza Hut uniform, which was too small. I was shocked to recognize him as the guy who had brought me a hamburger the day before, and I wondered what he was doing there. Obviously, he was shocked too, coming home from work and seeing me on what turned out to be his front porch. I guess we were destined to meet each other at every barbecue in Durango.

Someone came out and said we needed hamburger buns, so the guy—whose name, I learned, was Austin—nervously volunteered to go get them, and off he rode on his bike. When Austin came back with the buns, we had our first conversation. We found out we had both been to the same city in Tanzania, Africa, and talked about various things God was teaching us.

Our third encounter happened the next day, when a friend and I went to a worship night at a ranch in the mountains. On the beautiful drive up the mountainside, the trees seemed so vibrant, and I kept wondering and dreaming of what it would be like to have a ministry in a place like that and get to make that beautiful drive regularly. The singing started shortly after we arrived, and that was when I noticed that Austin was also there. I couldn't believe it. I wondered how he even knew the people who had invited me. He turned around and noticed me too.

After the event, Austin ended up riding home with us, so we had yet more time to get to know each other on the forty-minute drive.

These divine appointments happened for five days. But then Austin decided to take matters into his own hands by setting up one of these "happenstance" meetings. He brought his guitar with him so he could "just happen to be walking by" when I got off work and play it for me.

On his way, though, the Lord convicted Austin of not trusting Him with me and our new friendship. Just then, he saw a guy on the side of the road with a sign that said, "How can I pray for you?" Austin stopped his ten-speed to pray. They prayed together so long that he was convinced he'd missed me, so he got back onto his bike. But that day, I happened to get off work late, and I walked out just as he was turning for home.

You can guess the rest of the story. Six months later, we were married.

Ten years and half a dozen kids later, while we were both on staff with Master Plan Ministries, a man approached the founder of Master Plan saying he wanted to donate the very ranch where Austin and I had met for the third time. The ranch needed a ton of work, but God worked out the details so that another ministry owned it and let us use it free of charge while we renovated it.

Our ministry does a lot of Great Commission training at conferences and retreats, so the ranch became an incredibly strategic tool for us. It's a place where people can be trained and sent out, a greenhouse for discipleship where they can get into God's

Word, build relationships, learn to share the gospel and live on mission, and have fun without regret.

After the renovation was complete, the nonprofit that owned it said they would like our ministry to buy them out. We had one year to raise $1.85 million. I couldn't even wrap my mind around how much that was, but we needed to come up with it in 365 days. Then COVID-19 hit. Raising almost $2 million seemed 100 percent impossible at the best of times, and then it was exacerbated by having to do it when few people were receiving the same income. But God showed off. He did it. All the money came in. My mind is still blown.

Before God provided in this giant way, He gave us plenty of opportunities to trust Him with smaller things. For instance, when Austin and I were first married, we didn't have a car, so we prayed and prayed. Not long after, we had not one but two cars given to us! And this happened with all kinds of furniture and musical instruments too.

With little income, we had to rely first on prayer rather than our budget. So when the Lord led us to move closer to the college campus where we did ministry, we knew that if He really was leading, He would provide us a place to live. We put our house on the market and quickly had a full-price offer.

Then we turned to finding a home in Denver. The housing market there was beginning to boom, so it was the norm to give a full-price offer in order to beat out any competitors. Sometimes, there were even over-asking-price offers. We looked at a few places that were in our price range, but they were just too small for our growing family.

One day, after looking at yet another house that was too small, we noticed that the house across the street from it was for sale. It was gorgeous, so I immediately dismissed it, knowing it had to be out of our price range. I didn't want to waste my time looking at something we couldn't afford. But my husband and our Realtor proved to have more faith than I did.

We went to see the house, and it turned out to be exactly what we needed, not only for our family but also for the ministry. It was a five-minute drive from campus and had two separate living rooms that could be used for simultaneous men's and women's

Bible studies. Our kids could have their own area in the house, and the backyard was twice as big as the other lots, which would be great for large groups. But, as you would expect, it was $60,000 over what we could afford.

Our only source of encouragement was that the owners had displayed Scripture in various places around their house. That might seem normal if you lived in the Bible Belt, but this was in highly unchurched Denver. So we made an offer with all the money we could muster and wrote a letter explaining why we were moving and wanted this house.

Now rewind two weeks. The owner of the house had lived there twenty years, and for every week of those twenty years, she had hosted a prayer meeting. This was a ministry house, and yet it was too big, and she needed to move. The owner put her house on the market, praying it would still be used for ministry. At one point, she started to worry about the money, but the Lord told her that someone was going to put an offer on the house and that she should take the offer without worrying about it.

Then our offer and letter came in. Needless to say, she took our (below-asking-price) offer. She even gave testimony at her church, praising God for how we had come along with the offer. This dear lady had practically given us $60,000—and then praised God for us!

Walking into opportunities the Lord gave us, like this one, and seeing Him show off have greatly increased our faith.

But what about when it doesn't seem like God is providing? What about when money, resources, or people are lacking? Lots of believers have felt like that: for instance, the disciples. They walked around with Jesus, God in the flesh, and then He died. They didn't have the luxury of seeing ahead, so for those three days they were devastated. Their hope for the future, the hope of the world, was crushed. In those three days, they must have thought God's plan had been snuffed out.

Sometimes, we can get stuck in those three days and think God hasn't provided or that He has failed or didn't measure up or doesn't care. We can believe the same lies that the disciples may have believed. But really, He just hasn't completed His plan.

Perhaps His provision hasn't been fulfilled yet. Second Peter 3:9 tells us that He is not slow; He's just patient. We can be so rushed and want things right now. But God is not like that. He sees the whole 3D puzzle when we see only one tiny piece.

We can have complete and total confidence in God to provide what we need when we need it, because it's His glory at stake. He is the provider. He can't *not* provide. It's who He is. Check out one of my favorite verses: "May God be gracious to us and bless us and make his face shine on us—*so that* your ways may be known on earth, your salvation among all nations" (Ps. 67:1–2). God's gracious provision for us is more about Him making His character known than it is about us. He will never fail to provide for us, because He is the provider and reveals Himself as such.

It can be scary to trust God as your provider. Before He comes through, you're just left to wonder and wait. And who likes waiting? But waiting, like suffering, develops perseverance, and perseverance develops character, and character develops hope (see Rom. 5:3–4).

But not everyone understands that. I've heard people say things like "You just don't have enough faith" when others lack something or when they're in a waiting season. This is heartbreaking. God's provision is not about us or the amount of faith we have. After all, He said our teeny tiny faith in Him—faith as small as a mustard seed—can have a big impact (see Matt. 17:20).

The point is that we don't control God. We don't get to call the shots. Take Shadrach, Meshach, and Abednego, for example (see Dan. 3). They got in big trouble for praying to God and refusing to worship Nebuchadnezzar, and they were going to be killed for their faith. What would the provision of God look like here? Would it look like keeping them from the fiery furnace so they wouldn't have to go through hard things? Isn't that what we often hope for when we talk about God "coming through" for us?

No, in the case of those three young men, God's provision looked like giving them the courage to walk through it. It looked like giving them the strength and perspective to walk into the fire. And His provision looked like sustaining them through the torment. Though we may have idols of comfort, convenience, and painlessness, God does not. God's provision does not look like the American mindset of getting what we want when we want it so we'll be happy and safe.

God's provision often doesn't look like what we think it should. Sometimes His provision will be like it was for Shadrach, Meshach, and Abednego. In those times, it will be courage, sustaining grace, and perspective as we go through pain and sickness in this broken world.

One time I was discipling a girl with whom I had a pretty uncomfortable relationship. I relate the whole story later in this chapter, but right now I'll just say that God provided the words I needed at that time to help make a turn in that friendship. But admitting my sin to her was the last thing I wanted to do. And yet those hard words are the provision that God wanted to use to bring healing.

We live in a world that wants things immediately and easily. But God's ways are not our ways, and His thoughts are not our thoughts (see Isa. 55:9). His provision might look like walking through hard circumstances rather than around them. And His healing might come on the other side of eternity rather than in the timing we'd prefer. After all, God doesn't see space and time the same way we do. We may ask God to heal a sick relative, and yet he or she still dies. To us, that might look like God failing in some way. But the way God sees it, if the person was a believer, He did bring healing, just to a fuller degree than we were expecting. When that relative stepped from the broken world into heaven, he or she was fully healed.

The provision of God does not mean He is a candy dispenser. We don't get to choose *how* He provides—He does. We don't get to choose *when* He provides—He does. And His timing is full of so much more goodness and provision than what we even expect. "And God is able to bless you abundantly, so that in all things at all times, having all that you need, you will abound in every good work" (2 Cor. 9:8).

And one other important thing to point out is that God will provide for all your *needs*. "My God will meet all your *needs* according to the riches of his glory in Christ Jesus" (Phil. 4:19). This is different from all your *wants* (although He loves to hear those). And He knows our needs even before we do (see Matt. 6:8). Yet sometimes, He

The most exciting stories are on the other side of feeble steps of faith.

waits until *we* see the needs before He steps in and provides, just to give us a glimpse of His heart as a provider. There is no doubt He will provide for all your needs in the way and timing He sees fit, either in this life or the next.

I think God sometimes likes showing off as our provider. He likes it when we trust Him and He gets to show the *S* on His chest. Like when He told Moses to lead the Israelites out of Egypt. He told Moses He would be with him, and He came through every step of the way. He parted the Red Sea, He gave them manna and quail, and He kept their shoes from wearing out (see Deut. 8:2–4).

He also showed off when He told Joshua to be courageous and lead the people into the Promised Land, and when He told Gideon to deliver His people from the Midianites (see Josh. 1; Judg. 6). Each time, God told His people to do something and promised He would be with them, and then—*bam*—He showed off in how He came through for them.

In fact, did you know that every time God told someone in Scripture that He would be with him or her, He showed off? And He tells you the same thing: He will be with you. He tells you in Isaiah 43:1 not to fear and in Matthew 28:19–20 to take initiative to make disciples and He will be with you. When you step out in even a small act of faith and take God at His Word, He will always show up and show off, though His intervention might remain invisible to you. After all, look what God can do with a mustard seed. It's a tiny seed, and yet it brings forth a large tree (see Mark 4:31–32).

Last summer, my daughter Eden invited a girl from soccer to go to Awana with her. The girl ended up going to our church that weekend, along with her brother and mom. After church, I got to share the gospel with her, and she gave her life to Christ. God came through when Eden took a little step of faith and offered an invitation, and the impact rippled through eternity. And He will do the same for you.

You can live confidently and make faith decisions boldly because God will come through for you. You can step out in faith doing what God tells you to do because He will come through for you. The most exciting stories are on the other side of feeble steps of faith. You don't have to have it all figured out before taking your first step. Just take one step at a time. God loves showing off through even the tiniest bits of His people's faith.

"For the eyes of the LORD range throughout the earth to strengthen those whose hearts are fully committed to him" (2 Chron. 16:9).

# God Will Fight for You

Have you ever heard of glow worms? Not the stuffed animals from the eighties, but real glow worms. They live in caves in Australia, where they attach to the ceiling and let down glowing goo to lure insects. They are so beautiful and yet so horribly disgusting at the same time. They remind me of how Satan is described as an angel of light (see 2 Cor. 11:14).

So, get this: glow worms let out a light to deceive the prey they want to devour. They have a little bioluminescent taillight made by a chemical reaction between luciferin, a waste product, and the enzyme luciferase. When an insect is lured in and caught, the glow worm sucks it up and attaches it to a mucus tube to keep it from escaping.[1] Does it strike you as weird that this worm that parades as light to lure and kill has a chemical reaction between luciferin and luciferase?[2]

If this isn't a warning in creation, I don't know what is! Satan, the great deceiver— also known as Lucifer, which means "bearer of light"—offers what seems like life and pleasure, just as this worm does with its beguiling light. But in the end, his light leads to death.

Let us be wise, recognize his glowing goo, and not be lured by the attraction. Let's flee temptation by the strength of the Holy Spirit so we don't get trapped in a death machine. Death can begin with just one glance, which starts the progression James describes: "Each person is tempted when they are dragged away by their own evil desire and enticed. Then, after desire has conceived, it gives birth to sin; and sin, when it is full-grown, gives birth to death" (1:14–15). Death begins at the conception of desire, in the thought life. Whatever you feed, grows, and death is never satisfied.

It's the same with dogs. Imagine you have two dogs and you feed one and starve the other. If they get into a fight, which one do you think will win? The one you've fed.

In our ministry to help students grow, we do something called "soul to souls." A soul-to-soul talk is when a small group of girls share their life stories with one another. The goal is vulnerability, so many times girls share things they have never shared with anyone. Yet every time I hear their stories, I am struck by the similarities of their struggles. No two stories are exactly the same, but there truly is no struggle or temptation that no one else struggles with (see 1 Cor. 10:13). We are all in this battle together.

The lure of the Enemy is strong. The lie of "Just one bite; then I'll be satisfied" is so easy to believe. But that bite is the beginning of death.

So what is *your* glowing goo? What is the lure that seems to always catch you? Lies grow in the dark, but God's light brings healing. Are you willing to bring your goo into the light? Are you willing to share with a close friend how you are struggling? Growth comes when we share the junk in our hearts and see that we are still loved and accepted. And freedom comes when lies are exposed.

First Peter 5:8 tells us to be self-controlled and alert because we have an unseen Enemy prowling around seeking to devour us. His poison is lies. His schemes are tailor-made just for you. You *are* in a battle, whether you see it, feel it, think so, or not. Yet God has equipped you with everything you need. He's given you weapons of divine power to fight every excuse, thought, or rationalization that holds itself up against what God says is true. You are equipped to fend off lies about God, yourself, and others. He has given you truth, His Word, His righteousness, salvation, readiness to share the gospel, and faith. These are the armor and weapons described in Ephesians 6.

What we believe about God is the most important thing about us, so it's a good thing that God reveals His character to us. If He didn't show us what He was like, we wouldn't be able to see or know Him. But believing truth about Him takes effort and practice. Belief doesn't naturally happen, especially when the stakes are high.

Hebrews 5:14 describes maturity as being able to discern truth from error by letting God train our senses. We need to take every thought captive (see 2 Cor. 10:5), but how will we know which thoughts are lies and need to be taken captive if we are not in God's Word?

We desperately need quality time with the Lord in His Word, and a battle is raging to keep us from it. Personally, what keeps me from that quality time is going to bed too late because I'm doing some little thing that really can wait until the next day. What is it for you? What keeps you from having regular quality time with the Lord? Fight the battle there.

Let me tell you a rather embarrassing story. Why? Well, because I want to make sure I don't hold myself up as the hero rather than Jesus. So what better way to do that than to give you a glimpse of some of the yuck that can come out of me?

When the boys were little, I loved taking them to the Children's Museum of Denver. There were so many great things for them to do and learn. It had a jungle room, a fire truck, a veterinary office, a little grocery store, a bubble room, a train room … basically, it was a kid's dream. One day while the boys were playing on the fire truck, Uriah hit a little girl because she wouldn't share with him. He couldn't have been more than three years old. Obviously, it's not okay for him to go around hitting people. He knew that, and I totally would have addressed it.

However, I found out about the incident when I heard some woman yelling at my child. Hello, Mama Bear. I picked up Uriah (since he was bawling his head off from being yelled at by a stranger) and walked over to Austin.

Okay, get ready for the "whatever you feed, grows" part.

I commented to Austin about the woman's behavior, "That is crazy. You just can't do that." There was something about just saying it aloud that made me even madder. So I said it again, loud enough that everyone could hear, and it fed my flesh even more: "You just can't yell at someone else's kid!"

The other mom overheard me. "You got a problem?" she said, matching my sass.

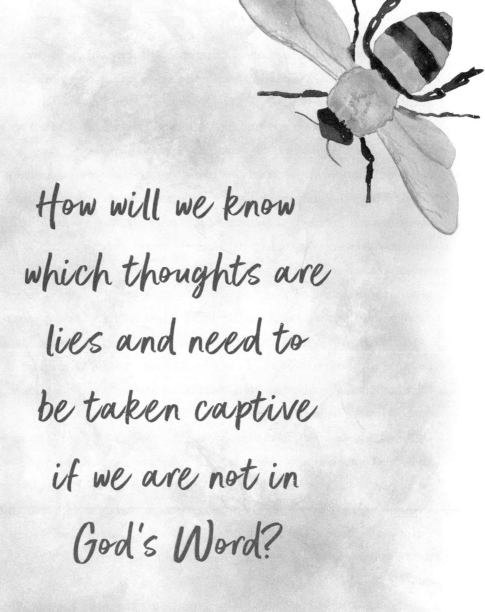

How will we know
which thoughts are
lies and need to
be taken captive
if we are not in
God's Word?

Well, my flesh was fully fed, and right there in the children's museum, there was a yelling match in front of all the three- and four-year-olds. Me, a missionary, was yelling at this lady!

Seriously, how embarrassing! Austin stepped in with his wise self and recovered the situation. He talked with the lady and helped Uriah apologize. I was so ashamed of my behavior. I honestly can't remember being that humiliated in a really long time.

So what's the point of this story, besides giving you an opportunity to feel good about yourself because you've probably never gotten into a screaming match at a kids' play area? It's this: We are in a battle where Satan's fiery lies are being thrown. And if we don't take our thoughts and speculations captive, they will give birth to sin, and sin gives birth to death.

We don't have to look far to find "nasty" and "awful." They're right inside us, waiting to master us. "Sin is crouching at your door; it desires to have you, but you must rule over it" (Gen. 4:7). You and I need to be alert and ready, on guard against not only the Enemy but also our flesh, which desires to have its way. Let's cling to Jesus and call out to Him for help, taking every yucky thought captive.

The flesh is tricky and can easily deceive us. After all, "the heart is deceitful above all things" (Jer. 17:9). So how can we tell if we are deceiving ourselves? God built into us a great little thing to show us what's going on in our hearts: our actions. When we are not being gentle, self-controlled, patient, kind, loving, and displaying other qualities of Christ, it's an indication—a blinking alarm light, so to speak—pointing to something that is not right in our hearts or our perceptions, which can be fixed only by seeing God as He truly is.

The things that come out of our mouths are from the heart (see Mark 7:14–23). Our words, attitudes, and behaviors give us a peek into what is going on inside us. Or, more realistically, a peek into who we are letting take charge of our lives. The fruit of the Spirit is just that: the fruit of the *Spirit*. Not the fruit of our own awesomeness. Therefore, we can see this fruit as a thermometer of the heart to tell us if we are yielding to the Lord or if we have self on the throne of our hearts.

If the spiritual fruit gauge on the dashboard of your life is showing an empty gas tank, you need to tend to the problem. Take a minute to confess your sin to God and surrender to His way, allowing Him to live His life through you.

But what about our feelings? We can't just ignore them. Our feelings are a gift from God, though they may not always feel that way. They allow us to understand a little more of what Jesus must have felt when He was rejected by those He ministered to … and when He was betrayed by a friend. But our feelings also connect us to the joy Jesus felt when He saw new spiritual life and shared great affection with close friends.

However, as with many things in life, it's very easy to make emotions the center of our existence and try to live in such a way that we experience never-ending good emotions, avoiding the bad. It's so easy to idolize our emotions, make our purpose to be happy, and let our feelings be the ultimate authority on what we do with our time. Instead of making our emotions our authority, we need to repeatedly remind ourselves of what is true about God, regardless of how we feel and regardless of our circumstances.

Since we're on the topic of this spiritual battle and the Enemy, I want to remind you that Satan doesn't have ultimate authority. Remember Job? God was bragging about him and his faith, and Satan had to ask permission to take away his family and livelihood. This shows that God had the ultimate authority. I think we forget that sometimes.

One time, I was in a store, and as often happens when I walk up to a register, the cashier said, "Whoa. I'm sorry, but something just happened to the register. Hang on; let me fix it." I proceeded to tell her that I hear those words about half the time when I walk up to some piece of technology (no joke). I told her that God uses it to teach me patience. That got her all riled up, and she said, "This is not God; this is Satan!"

Satan is not in charge; God is. Satan might very well be carrying out a scheming plan, but if so, he had to ask permission first. God's got us. We might be pushed beyond what we think we're capable of handling, but we won't be pushed beyond what *He* is capable of handling. We are called to be strong in *His* mighty power, not ours (see Eph. 6:10).

You may remember that in chapter 1 I talked about Zephaniah 3:17, which describes God as a mighty warrior who saves. The verse shows the Lord as a warrior who is not worried, scared, timid, or uncertain about whether He's going to win. He *knows* He's going to win. We already established that He knows all things. Our God is so confident in His ability that you can rest and make your worries known to Him, fully assured that He will fight for you. And He will win.

In Acts 12, we see God fighting for Peter while Mary and a houseful of people are praying for him. God sends an angel to lead Peter out of jail to the very place they are praying. Rhoda, a servant girl, is so shocked she runs to tell the others without even letting Peter in the house. God is still in the business of leading people out of prison, but today it often looks different. Instead of bondage in a jail cell, we deal with the bondage of lies about self, others, and God.

God is not distant or uninvolved. He is the defender of the weak and will come to your defense. When you yield to Him, He will do through you what only He can do. At the end of your life, when you're standing before the God who passionately cares for you, it will be beyond obvious that He never let you down. Hang tight, friend. He fights for you.

"The LORD will fight for you; you need only to be still" (Ex. 14:14).

## God Will Lead You in Truth

When I was first on staff with Master Plan Ministries, I didn't have kids, which meant I had gobs of time, so I discipled a lot of girls. Each week, I met with the student leaders individually to get into God's Word with them and to provide some ministry training.

Two of the girls didn't seem to care for me that much. While others begged to meet with me, these two sat back with their arms crossed and smug looks on their faces, communicating to me with their body language, *Just see if you can teach us anything.* I was beyond intimidated. I wasn't that much older than them and didn't have much more experience. I dreaded our times together and pleaded with the Lord to show me what to say before each meeting.

One day, the Lord led me to share with one of these girls something I was struggling with. Now, it's just scary to share something very personal with someone who doesn't think very highly of you and who might use it against you! Well, I did it anyway, and the craziest thing happened. She started crying.

As we sat across the table from each other, and with tears dribbling down her cheeks, she said that what I'd shared was the exact same thing she was struggling with. I was stunned. That moment changed our friendship. She is now one of my closest friends and someone I absolutely adore. The truth sets people free.

There's another story about the truth setting someone free. John 4 tells her story.

Let me pause for a second and point out that even the reality that John 4 tells her story is "wow" worthy. The God who created soapsuds and the thorny lizard, the One who breathed the stars into being, thinks this beautiful lady's story is worth sharing, so He moved John to write it down so that we who live now can read it. This is the longest recorded conversation in Scripture between Jesus and anyone. And the fact that the Lord made sure His longest documented conversation with anyone was with a woman—an outcast woman, no less—is flat-out shocking. God thinks this story is a big deal.

This John 4 lady was vulnerable and disregarded. She was a social outcast not known to us by her name but by her location and her sin. But Jesus stepped in and changed that. He spoke hard truth and ridiculous grace.[3] He honored her and ended her story with eternal redemption, and John later bragged about how many people came to know Jesus because of her.

This lady is known as the adulterous woman at the well. Jesus talked to her when no one else would. Even the disciples were embarrassed He was talking to her. He began by talking with her about water but quickly got personal, asking her to go get her husband. Respectable women didn't speak with a man alone in public. So when Jesus asked her to get her husband, He was honoring her, assuring her of His interest in her welfare. He revealed that He knew all about her sin and that He was the Messiah, the One she was looking for.

He is so good at speaking truth in love. As He did with her, God always tells the truth, and the truth will set you free (see John 8:31–32).

Hebrews 12 tells us that God is like a good father who disciplines the children he loves. We are often sinful, and our flesh convinces us of things that are not true about God, ourselves, and others. And yet, God is incredibly wise and gracious in how He leads us back to the truth.

We see Him in action when He deals with David, who had a relationship with a married woman and then killed her husband to cover it up (see 2 Sam. 11). God sends Nathan to address David's sin and bring him to repentance. But He doesn't blast him. God has Nathan tell David a story about a man who stole a guy's only sheep, although he had a ton of his own. As David gets angry about the injustice, Nathan reveals that *David* is that man.

"Then David said to Nathan, 'I have sinned against the LORD.' Nathan replied, 'The LORD has taken away your sin. You are not going to die. But because by doing this you have shown utter contempt for the LORD, the son born to you will die'" (12:13–14).

So David admits his sin and turns from it, and the Lord is gracious to forgive, although there would still be serious consequences.

There is another example of someone in Scripture being corrected and led to the truth, but this person responds very differently. In 1 Samuel 15, God tells Saul to completely destroy the Amalekites. Saul does so, but not all the way. His soldiers defeat the Amalekites and destroy much of their property, but they save the best plunder, and they keep the king around.

Saul's decision ended up causing devastating consequences for the Jews. Centuries later, Haman, the one who was determined to annihilate the Jews in the book of Esther, was an Amalekite.

Anyway, Saul didn't fully obey the Lord. Rather, he did what he wanted and what was right in his own eyes. He obeyed just enough to think he'd actually done what God wanted. He kept the best of the sheep and cattle and everything that was good, but somehow, he still totally believed he did an amazing job obeying God. It reminds me of how kids "sort of" obey. They shove everything in the closet and then look so proud about cleaning their rooms. In fact, Saul was so proud of himself that he made a monument in his own honor. Face-palm moment.

When Samuel arrived, Saul actually began to brag about what a great job he'd done. God used Samuel to correct him and lead him to the truth. When Samuel asked why he didn't fully obey, Saul kept up the whole "I did" act. But when Samuel pointed out the specifics, Saul started pointing his finger, saying it was the soldiers' fault (see v. 21). It took a few tries to sink into Saul's thick head, but finally when he heard the consequences of his actions, his attitude changed and he started admitting he disobeyed because he was afraid of his soldiers. He apologized and asked Samuel to honor him before the men.

We don't know Saul's heart, but it sure seems like he cared way more about being honored by others than he did about honoring God. It seems like he cared way more about what others thought of him than what God thought of him. And he didn't even admit he'd done anything wrong until he heard the consequences. God led him to the truth, but it seems Saul chose to reject it. When he did finally admit his failure, it wasn't even a full admission but a plea to get out of the consequences.

God will lead us to truth and expose any lies we believe, but then we have a choice to make: Will we believe Him? When we are corrected, we can blame-shift, rationalize, downplay our mistakes, or explain why we just *had* to do it … or we can take responsibility and repent.

Genuine repentance is always preceded by awareness of sin, which is followed by conviction. True repentance is admitting where we have disobeyed God and turning from our sin. There are no excuses and no blaming. Since God is a shepherd who leads His people, we can probably count on Him to lead us to places that most likely will require us to deny our flesh, take up our crosses, and follow Him. But He will give hard truth with ridiculous grace.

God deeply cares for you. He will always lead you gently in truth, fight for you, and come through for you as you step out in faith and trust Him.

"Since my youth, God, you have taught me, and to this day I declare your marvelous deeds" (Ps. 71:17).

# CONNECT WITH THE LORD

Watch the chapter 5 video now. Find the video using the QR code or link on page 22.

## God Will Come Through for You, Fight for You, and Lead You

• What do these verses say about truth?

Proverbs 12:17

John 14:6

John 16:13

Ephesians 4:15

2 Timothy 4:4

• Which verse sticks out the most to you, and why?

## Truth Chart

| | |
|---|---|
| • 1. In what ways have you felt trapped or defenseless? | • 6. What is one way you can act on what is true? |
| • 2. How is it impacting your life: feelings, thoughts, choices? | • 5. If you believed God would *lead you*, how would it impact your wants and actions? |
| • 3. What does it show that you believe about God? | • 4. If you truly believed God *cared about you*, how would it impact your feelings? |

Chapter 6

# You Can't Mess Up God's Plan

We waited for answers as we sat by the hospital bed where my four-year-old girl was strapped down so she wouldn't yank out her breathing tube. She was having seizures and hallucinations, and she and I would spend three weeks in the ICU of a children's hospital.

Ultimately, she had to receive a blood plasma transfer, which is when they put a tube through the artery in her neck to her heart that took out her blood, separated and cleaned the plasma, and put it back in.

During those three weeks, I experienced dramatic highs and lows. I saw God comfort and care for us through the support of the body of Christ, and I felt deep, wrenching pain when my daughter didn't recognize me. Once, she hallucinated I was a monster trying to get her as she cried out for me. I desperately wanted to hold her, but she saw me as someone else and was left feeling alone and abandoned.

Not long before this, Austin and I had received a diagnosis that two of our boys had a serious mental illness. Their explosive anger came as quickly as turning on a faucet, and it happened over minor things like what was for dinner. Dealing with their daily, sometimes hours-long explosions made the hospital stay feel like a welcome retreat. We were in a season of constant dependence on Jesus, trying to figure out how to get each kid the help he or she needed.

The boys' constant irritability and opposition had brought us to a depth of desperation for Jesus that I didn't know was possible, and it exposed deep-down doubts about God that we'd never have known about if all this hadn't happened. The combination of the boys' outbursts and my little girl's time in the hospital brought thoughts to my mind I'd never had. Thoughts like, *Is God powerless? Is He weak? Is His arm too short to save?* The experience brought lies out of darkness and into the light. The good thing is that when lies are brought into the light, they can be exposed for what they are—lies—rather than growing ever more pungent in darkness.

Maybe your "hard" isn't in the form of an ER room or a mental illness, but it is still all too real. Perhaps your "unexpected" has brought to your mind thoughts about God you've never thought before. The propensity to believe untrue things about God has always been in us, but perhaps the opportunity to believe them was not. God cares and loves us enough to expose the parts of us that will hurt us and others. Perhaps your situation is the means God wants to use to root out the lies you believe about Him. Perhaps what you believe about Him is so important that He would allow the unexpected and hard you're going through to expose lies, as He did with me.

"The crucible for silver and the furnace for gold, but the LORD tests the heart" (Prov. 17:3). Just as a crucible melts metals with intense heat to create something new and the smelter applies heat to extract base metals and burn away impurities, so the Lord uses suffering and challenges to purify our hearts and minds and to extinguish lies we believe about Him.

When a goldsmith works with gold, he first needs to put it in the fire to refine it. While it's in the fire, the impurities rise to the surface, and he scrapes them off. The process is repeated several times until the goldsmith can see his reflection in the gold. The Lord is our goldsmith, and we are the gold. He uses the pain in this life as His smelter to surface and remove impurities we didn't even know were there.

The Lord is our goldsmith, and we are the gold. He uses the pain in this life as His smelter to surface and remove impurities we didn't even know were there.

Hebrews 12 tells us the Lord disciplines the ones He loves. The truth is, He loves us so deeply that He's unwilling to let us stay the way we are—or to believe the lies we believe. And the suffering He allows to refine us isn't worth comparing to the glory that will be revealed in us (see Rom. 8:18).

Now, some believe that any suffering we endure is a sign that God is not strong enough to prevent it. But just because God allows us to stay in the pain for our own growth and refinement (as well as for His glory), it doesn't make Him any less powerful. In fact, perhaps His power is demonstrated all the more when He doesn't step in and pull us out of our pain.

It's easy to have an overinflated view of ourselves, thinking we need to do X or God won't be able to do Y. But God does not need us, and He can't be stopped by us. We can no more mess up the plan of God than an ant can mess up builders constructing a multimillion-dollar home. And that example is not even a wide-enough expanse to show the distance between God's knowledge and ability and ours. God is completely self-sufficient.

Let's zoom in on this a bit. God has never needed anyone or anything, ever. He has always existed and been fully complete in every way, forever. Our brains can't *fully* grasp this concept, but they can just a little, so let's push the limit. God is eternal. That means He will exist forever. He will not only exist forever in the future, but He has always existed in the past. Before the world, He was. He was the One who spoke into existence the elements of what we see. He also has no end. He has no bounds, no limit to who He is.

Now, who is He? What is He like? Surely there is an end to His characteristics or attributes, such as love, generosity, kindness, faithfulness, and goodness. Surely we can come to the end of those. Surely we can count all His good attributes and reach the end of them after 3,529 or so.

No! We could spend every day of our entire lives counting the amazing things about God and not finish. And let's not stop there. Even if we kept counting for all eternity, we would never come to the end of even just *naming* the amazing truths about God, let alone learning about them.

Is your mind blown yet? Oh, don't you just love meditating on God!

Let's keep going. Not only can we not fully grasp how big and unending God is, but we also can't grasp how wide He is. Let's try, because isn't seeking God one of life's greatest treasures? Let's take just one of His attributes, say, love or goodness. Can we ever come to the end of God's love or reach the edge of His goodness? Surely it will one day be all used up so there will not be enough for us. Never! All of who God is has always been, always will be, and can never be diminished. His love for you before you were even formed was just as strong and deep as it is now—and it will be the same a thousand years from now.

All the nations are just "a drop in a bucket" to God (Isa. 40:15). If all people who have ever existed across all time haven't depleted the goodness, kindness, love, justice, and an eternity of other attributes of God, then why should we think He will run out when it comes to us?

You can spend eternity learning about just one attribute of God and never know all there is to know about it. God is eternal.

Here are a few lines from my favorite poem, which captures the emotions felt when thinking about the eternality of God:

> *And just when I think I know Your voice,*
> *You open up my ears.*
> *It's like trying to know every single glowing star on a cloudless night.*
> *But Your depth and Your vastness*
> *Keep me running after You.[1]*

Let's spend some time gazing at the power, knowledge, and artistry of God, which clearly display how we just can't mess up His plan.

# God Is Powerful

"In the beginning God created the heavens and the earth," and He said, "Let there be light" (Gen. 1:1, 3). And light came out of the mouth of God, so to speak, at roughly 186,000 miles per second.

Have you ever noticed that light was created before the sun, moon, and stars? Oh, how I love science. It's like God's art show. We get to learn more about Him by learning about what He's made. So on day one, God made light—photons, a building block of the universe. Photons and electromagnetic energy are the stuff which makes up all light. And then on day three, God made the sun, moon, and stars. He breathed out the sun at about 10,000 degrees Fahrenheit and 865,000 miles across. That's more than a hundred times as big as the earth.

I love total solar eclipses, especially those few moments when the moon completely blocks the light of the sun. Did you know that the moon is four hundred times smaller than the sun? You wouldn't think something that small could completely eclipse the sun. However, the moon is also four hundred times farther away from the sun than it is from the earth. That leaves both bodies with the same angular size, about one-half a degree, from the perspective of someone on earth.

This means that a total solar eclipse allows astronomers to study the sun's lower atmosphere, its chromosphere. If the moon were a sliver smaller, it would allow too much light and scientists couldn't see the chromosphere. And if the moon were a sliver bigger, it would block that part of the sun. This perfect proportion allows astronomers to understand how stars work and scientists to learn about light.

Okay, how crazy is this event in creation, where the radiance of the sun is blocked just enough that it gives us a glimpse of its atmosphere? Wow! This shouts Exodus 33:18 to me, when Moses calls out to the Lord, "Now show me your glory." He wants to see Him and know Him. And guess what God does: He answers Moses's request by promising to block His radiance so that Moses can see and understand His incredibleness (see vv. 19–23). He agrees to give Moses a glimpse of His patience, grace, and justice. The light would be blocked so he could learn.

Solar eclipses show us that God makes a way for us to know Him. He brings together all the right circumstances so we're able to get a glimpse of what He's really like, just as the sun's radiance being blocked by the moon gives us a glimpse that lets us understand its light. God wants to be known, and He is powerful enough to help us see and understand Him.

Paul prayed for the Ephesians to know God's "incomparably great power for us who believe" (1:19). So really, how powerful *is* God? Let's look at what He made. Jeremiah 10:12 says, "God made the earth by his power."

So this earth that God made by His power jogs around the sun at 18.5 miles per second. It orbits an average of 93 million miles away from the sun, which just so happens to be the exact place for life to flourish. If it were much closer, our water would boil and vaporize. Much farther, and our water would freeze solid. It has to be in the so-called habitable (or "Goldilocks") zone—not too close to the sun and not too far away.

Our planet also needs things like a moon that is roughly one-quarter the size of the earth so the gravitational pull stabilizes the angle of the axis, which keeps the seasons straight. It needs the right thickness in the planet's crust to regulate temperature. God also needed to make the earth with liquid iron at its core to generate a magnetic field. And He had to make it orbit a G2 main-sequence (dwarf) star so it wouldn't be knocked off its rotation into synchronization with the sun, causing only half of the earth to get sunlight.

The atmosphere also had to have the perfect ratio of nitrogen and oxygen to protect us from the sun's rays. The earth had to have liquid water (in correct ratio), a nearly circular orbit, the correct mass, plate tectonics, continents, and a moderate rate of rotation—among other things. When God made the earth, He had to exert His power so that more than twenty conditions were set exactly right in order for it to sustain your life.[2]

We can also see the power of God through the life of Christ. He is sustaining everything, upholding it by His Word. He raised Lazarus, a little girl, and Himself from the dead. He made the blind see, and He made limbs whole again. He healed a paralytic and a lady who'd had a bleeding disease for twelve years. He calmed wild waves, turned water to wine, and fed five thousand men (likely twenty thousand people including families). He stayed focused on His mission and would not be controlled by the tyranny of the urgent. Jesus kept Himself under control as He let people beat Him, spit on Him, pull out His beard, and nail Him to a cross. He walked on water, softened hard hearts, and fulfilled more than 330 prophecies.

Let's look at that one a bit more. According to Peter Stoner in his book, *Science Speaks*, the probability of those 330 prophecies being accidentally fulfilled in one man is astronomically low. Stoner calculated that the chances of one man randomly fulfilling even *eight* of those prophecies was 10 to the 17th power. That would be one chance in 100,000,000,000,000,000. Stoner wrote that this number could be compared to covering the state of Texas two feet deep with silver dollars, painting one of them red, and tossing it randomly into the pile, then putting a blindfold on your friend and telling her she has one chance to pick up that red one.[3]

That is the chance of only eight prophecies being fulfilled in one person by happenstance, and yet Jesus fulfilled more than 300—and others are yet to come! That is powerful.

He is powerful enough to not be controlled by His feelings and whims. He is powerful enough to not be controlled or manipulated by us toward our own destruction. He is powerful enough to not fly off the handle at us. He is powerful enough to know how to speak to us in ways we can understand and lead us to the truth. He is powerful enough to shape our desires and give us the mind of Christ.

And God is powerful enough to show His power through imperfect people. Isaiah says, "The LORD is the everlasting God, the Creator of the ends of the earth. He will not grow tired or weary, and his understanding no one can fathom. He gives strength to the weary and increases the power of the weak" (40:28–29).

Surely you and I can't mess up God's plan. He is far too powerful for that.

# God Knows All Things

A ministry team I was on asked everyone to take the Gallup StrengthsFinder test. It turned out my top strength was *learning*. At first, I was a bit disappointed. *Learning?* It felt so selfish. How could that help anyone? How could that glorify God? But as I get glimpses of how God uses me in various ways, I can see how this love and strength of learning does benefit others. After all, I am writing this book to share what God has shown me through the process of learning.

Anyway, I love aha moments. Some people like roller coasters or skydiving. I like having my mind blown. One of my favorite life-altering aha moments happened when I was in Nepal. But first, some backstory.

I came to Christ when I was eleven. I was a painfully shy girl who was terrified to talk to people. But I was in every activity you could think of, so I was around people a lot. I vividly remember being at a barbecue with other families and their kids. My parents told me to go talk to someone, and I froze as dread overcame me. "No!" I pleaded. They gave me the look. You know that you're-in-huge-trouble-if-you-don't-get-your-butt-over-there look. So I walked up to a girl at the food table and said hi. That right there was enough to make me bust out into a full-blown sweat. Tami was so kind and friendly, and she asked if I wanted to go run on top of some barrels with her. I went and actually had fun, and I lightened up a bit.

That day, she invited me to watch her in a Christmas play at her church. It turned out that her church was just a few blocks from our house. I can remember very little of the play or the schedule of events, but I do remember very clearly that during the singing of a worship song, I saw God's hand over the worship team. It seemed very normal, and it convinced me that God wanted me there. I told my mom I thought God wanted us to go to this church, and so we started going regularly.

One Sunday after the service, the pastor walked down the aisle to my mom and me. He said hello and then turned to me and asked if I had ever accepted Christ. I was absolutely clueless about what he was asking me, so I mumbled something incoherent

The truth that I could not live the Christian life in my own strength was the biggest aha of my life.

about how I believed in God. He invited us back to his office and proceeded to share the gospel with me. That day, I admitted my guilt before God and surrendered my life to Him. I was a new creation—and the fear of people that had engulfed me … vanished. I went from petrified to talk with people to wanting to befriend new kids at school. Truly, the fear that had gripped me was gone. God had freed me.

As a baby Christian, I really loved God and wanted to please Him. I figured I could if I just tried hard enough. So I made a little "good-o-meter" out of a paper plate; I stuck a pushpin through a paper arrow to attach it to the middle of the plate and marked degrees of "goodness." At the end of each day, I would turn the arrow to how good a Christian I'd been that day. In those younger years, I honestly thought I could live the Christian life in my own strength if I just tried hard enough. I even got mad at God for not just giving me a list of everything I should and shouldn't do. I thought if I just had a list, surely I could live up to it.

Fast-forward twenty years. I was in Nepal on a mission trip asking God what He wanted me to do that day when I wasn't doing the work we'd gone there to do. That day, like each day before, I believed He wanted me to read the Bible. It was during this extensive time in God's Word when the book of Galatians came alive to me. The truth that I could not live the Christian life in my own strength was the biggest aha of my life.

The goal wasn't to try harder to be a good Christian. The goal was to yield to the God who could live His goodness through me. Galatians says it this way: "Are you so foolish? After beginning by means of the Spirit, are you now trying to finish by means of the flesh?" (3:3). It was only the Holy Spirit—not my effort—who could make me more like Jesus. "So I say, walk by the Spirit, and you will not gratify the desires of the flesh" (5:16). I realized that if I yielded to Him, He would cause His amazing qualities to come out in me. Things like kindness, self-control, gentleness, faithfulness, and joy. God's knowledge of me drew and taught me, and He continues to teach me every day.

God knows everything. Let that sink in. He knows everything about everything. He knows exactly how many elements He is using to hold everything together. He knows how many drops are in the ocean. He knows when each mountain goat gives birth. He knows how to command the day, make the scorpion's tail, give the bird flight, and do a trillion other things we take for granted.

And He knows everything about you. Physically, mentally, emotionally, socially … everything. And not only you, but also your great-great-great-grandma, whom you don't even know. But God knows her. He knows everything about her. Why she made every decision she ever made, why she felt every feeling she ever felt, why she loved what she loved and hated what she hated. He knew her.

God knows you too. Nothing is hidden from Him, not even one strand of your hair. He knows every single one. And He knows each tear that has ever fallen from your eyes. He knows every need you have, even ones you don't know about. Do you remember those comforting verses in Matthew 6 about the birds and wildflowers and how God knows how to take care of them? They show us some pretty cool things about God.

Did you know God gave the wild tobacco plant secret chemical weapons? When an insect attacks, the plant ramps up a toxin called nicotine. Nicotine poisons anything that has a muscle.

So now it has survived and is not being eaten by bugs; however, here comes Mr. Caterpillar, who has no muscles. The plant's secret chemical weapon doesn't work on him. Now the plant is being eaten alive, and chances are that if nothing happens, the entire plant will be devoured in a couple of days. But as we know, wild tobacco plants still exist; they haven't all been eaten alive. Are you curious as to why? Well, because they have yet another secret weapon.

When Mr. Caterpillar's saliva gets on the wild tobacco plant's leaves, the plant releases an odor that is picked up by the very bugs that eat caterpillars. Basically, the plant sends out secret SOS scents and calls in reinforcements. Within hours, Mr. Bug comes along and gobbles up Mr. Caterpillar. And if that weren't enough, the plant also makes little lollipop-looking things called trichomes.[4] The caterpillar eats these yummy little treats, and twenty minutes later, the secret weapon kicks in—and Mr. Caterpillar himself now emits a smell that is very appetizing to Mr. Bug.[5]

Pretty amazing, right? But there are even more secret weapons.

Now here comes Mrs. Hawk Moth gathering nectar from the flower of the wild tobacco plant. And she lays up to two hundred eggs, which grow into tobacco-eating caterpillars. So if little wild tobacco plant is starting to get too many hawk moth eggs on it, it senses this and changes the shape of its flower from short and open to tall and narrow. Now Mrs. Hawk Moth can't get the pollen, so she goes off to look for other places to do so. And along comes Mrs. Hummingbird, whose beak fits perfectly inside the long flower, to gather the nectar.[6]

This little wildflower doesn't even have a brain, yet it has at least three defense mechanisms tailor-made for different predators. God knew and provided for this flower of the field long before it ever even existed.

No wonder God tells us to consider the wildflowers (see Matt. 6:28). Wildflowers show us that God knows—He really, really knows. And not only does He know what is needed long before we ever see the need, but He also provides. In the same way He knew that the wild tobacco plant would need to ward off enemies and He provided the means, He also knew what you need and has set out to provide for you. He acts on your behalf. Abundantly.

Sin and brokenness haven't hindered His plan for your life. After all, no plan of His can be thwarted. It can be detoured but not messed up beyond repair. He is so big that your finite choices cannot alter the ultimate plan of an infinite, all-knowing, and powerful God. Because He knows all things, He knows how to keep His plan from unraveling. And if He cares enough to help a plant fight a caterpillar, then He surely cares much more for you, a valuable being created in His image.

Read through Matthew 6 thoughtfully; I've provided a couple of insights to help you apply it.

> Therefore I tell you, do not worry about your life, what you will eat or drink; or about your body, what you will wear. Is not life more than food, and the body more than clothes? Look at the birds of the air;

they do not sow or reap or store away in barns, and yet your heavenly Father feeds them. Are you not much more valuable than they? Can any one of you by worrying add a single hour to your life?

And why do you worry about clothes? See how the flowers of the field grow. They do not labor or spin. [They don't even have brains, let alone the ability to provide for themselves.] Yet I tell you that not even Solomon in all his splendor was dressed like one of these. [Could you imagine Solomon's soldiers having odor-releasing chemical weapons?] If that is how God clothes the grass of the field, which is here today and tomorrow is thrown into the fire, will he not much more clothe you—you of little faith? So do not worry, saying, "What shall we eat?" or "What shall we drink?" or "What shall we wear?" For the pagans run after all these things, and your heavenly Father knows that you need them. But seek first his kingdom and his righteousness, and all these things will be given to you as well. (vv. 25–33)

God knows everything. And any time *we* know something, it's because God gave us minds for understanding—brains that work and process information. His common grace gives wisdom and understanding generously to those who seek and ask Him.

God not only reveals knowledge, but He also conceals it. Austin and I were discussing what information we would and would not tell our kids at each stage in their lives. We concluded that we would withhold from them any information that would bring them harm. I think God is the same. He does not tell us everything, keeping from us those things that would harm us.

He also hides knowledge to woo us into seeking Him. We see this in Jesus' use of parables. The stories were sometimes confusing, which caused the disciples to go to Jesus and ask Him about His meaning. They even asked, "Why do you speak to the people in parables?" (Matt. 13:10). Jesus would often hide knowledge to get people to seek Him. He doesn't just toss His knowledge around and hope it sticks somewhere. He waits for us to call to Him and seek it.

Jeremiah 33:3 is another of my favorite verses: "Call to me and I will answer you and tell you great and unsearchable things you do not know." Is your mind blown? God *wants* to give us knowledge, understanding, and wisdom. Great, unsearchable knowledge. And all we have to do is go to Him for it.

We have been given the Holy Spirit, the very Spirit of God. He is the teacher, the revealer of truth, and the One who gives understanding, insight, discernment, and revelation. The truths you already know are in your mind because God gave you the ability to understand—and because He uncovered them for you. And He wants to teach you more if you would only call to Him.

## God Is a Master Craftsman

Diamonds are beautiful, and yet they are the hardest substance on earth. Only another diamond can break them. They are made from pure carbon, and when they are put under extreme pressure and scorching temperatures, the carbon atoms begin growing crystals, which cling together in extremely hard bonds. Through the refining process, these rough structures can be turned into beautiful gemstones.

That is what God does with us. He allows pressure and stress. He allows us to be "hard pressed on every side, but not crushed" (2 Cor. 4:8). Then He refines and polishes us. He uses the pressures of life to birth something beautiful and unbreakable. Our God is a master craftsman. His art is all around us in the clouds, colors, mountains, rivers, oceans, seashells, flowers, and even us, and though we can see some aspect of beauty, we are ignorant of much of it.

There is a fascinating pattern in nature called the divine proportion, or the golden ratio. It is a mathematical design element that is seen in creation in objects ranging from galaxies to atoms, from seashells to the number of petals on a flower. It is both aesthetically appealing and functional. It is constructed through something called the Fibonacci sequence, a series in which each number is the sum of the two that precede it. For example: 0+1=1, 1+1=2, 1+2=3, 2+3=5, 3+5=8, and so on; the sequence 0, 1, 1, 2, 3, 5, 8, 13, 21, 34, and so on. This pattern can be seen in many aspects of creation, showing that God is a master designer in everything He makes.

One of the places we see this sequence is in our galaxy. So let's consider it and see God's creative power. We live on one of eight planets that revolve around the sun. Our sun, the dominant light of our solar system, gives off far more energy in one second than all mankind has produced since creation.[7] And our sun is just one among 100 billion stars in our galaxy, the Milky Way. The Milky Way is so big that it takes 100,000 light years to travel from one side of it to the other. (One light year is 5.88 trillion miles, or the distance light travels in one year.) If the Milky Way were the size of North America, our solar system would be the size of a coffee cup.[8]

Isaiah wrote, "Lift up your eyes and look to the heavens: Who created all these? He who brings out the starry host one by one and calls forth each of them by name. Because of his great power and mighty strength, not one of them is missing" (40:26). Scientists estimate that there are one septillion stars in the universe (that's a one with twenty-four zeroes after it), many more stars than there are grains of sand on all of our planet's seashores (estimated at five sextillion grains—a five followed by twenty-one zeroes).[9] If all the stars were divided equally among the people of the world, each person would receive almost 125 trillion stars.

David tells us a beautiful thing about these stars: "The heavens declare the glory of God; the skies proclaim the work of his hands. Day after day they pour forth speech; night after night they reveal knowledge. They have no speech, they use no words; no sound is heard from them. Yet their voice goes out into all the earth, their words to the ends of the world" (Ps. 19:1–4). You may be wondering how this could be. What does David mean? How does the sky proclaim God's character and glory night after night? Get ready to have your mind blown again.

Adam named the animals, right? But God named the stars (see Ps. 147:4). Some of the brightest stars we see in the sky have been grouped into pictures called constellations. There are twelve main constellations that make up what the book of Job calls Mazzaroth (see 38:32 ESV). A more familiar term to us is *zodiac*, but we're not talking about horoscopes or astrology, which are distortions of what God artistically displayed about Himself. Those are schemes of the Enemy to twist something God made so that it's all about us instead of God. Rather, the Mazzaroth talked about in the Bible is all about Jesus.

Let's look at some of God's Word and see what God says about the stars. Here's what He says about the Mazzaroth in Job 38:31–32: "Can you bind the chains of the Pleiades [a star cluster in Taurus]? Can you loosen Orion's belt [in the Orion constellation]? Can you bring forth the constellations [the Hebrew word *mazzārâ*] in their seasons?"[10] Job is often thought to be the oldest book in the Bible, the first book written down. So the constellations that we know now were also known way back then, and they have been virtually unchanged. Taurus and Ursa Major, for example, appear in cave art.[11]

Also, the names of the stars have retained their meanings in various languages. For instance, the constellation Virgo is referred to as *bethulah* in Hebrew, *parthenos* in Greek mythology, and *kanya* in Hindi, all of which mean "virgin." This shows us there was knowledge of the names of the stars and constellations before the confusion and separation at the tower of Babel.

In Genesis 15:5, we see God "took [Abram] outside and said, 'Look up at the sky and count the stars—if indeed you can count them.'" The Hebrew word for "count" here is *saphar*, which means "to recount, to relate, to count."[12] "Then he said to him, 'So shall your offspring be.'" There was something about the stars that God used to remind Abram of the hope of God's plan.

So let's look at just one of the masterfully designed constellations. Virgo (the virgin) is depicted as holding wheat in her left hand and a branch in her right hand. The star on her left hand is named Spica, which in Latin and Hebrew means "the promised seed" or "the seed of the One who comes."[13] The star on her shoulder is named Zavijaveh, which means "beautiful Lord" in Hebrew.[14] And the star in her right hand, the one holding the branch, is Vindemiatrix, a Chaldee word that means "the son," or "branch, who cometh." It's also known as Al Mureddin, which means "who shall come down" or "who shall have dominion."[15]

So what we see in the constellation Virgo is a virgin holding the seed of one who comes, the beautiful Lord. Another star in Virgo is Al Tzemech, which means "branch." In the form *tsemech,* it is the Hebrew word used uniquely of the Messiah in many places in Scripture (such as Isa. 4:2; Jer. 23:5–6; 33:15; Zech. 3:8; 6:12).[16] The stars, which were named by God, point us to Jesus and His grand plan and story.

God masterfully fashions things to declare His glory. He is a God who cares for us passionately. He knows all things and has all power to do as He pleases, and He does things in a beautiful way.

"Why, my soul, are you downcast? Why so disturbed within me? Put your hope in God, for I will yet praise him, my Savior and my God" (Ps. 43:5).

# CONNECT WITH THE LORD

Watch the chapter 6 video now. Find the video using the QR code or link on page 22.

## God Is Powerful, Knows All Things, and Is a Master Craftsman

• What do these passages tell you about God?

Job 37:23

Job 42:1–2

Psalm 139:13–18

Psalm 147:5

Isaiah 14:27

Jeremiah 32:27

Matthew 19:26

Ephesians 1:19

- Which verse sticks out the most to you, and why?

## Truth Chart

| | |
|---|---|
| • 1. In what ways have you recently felt like God was powerless or didn't know what you needed? | • 6. What is one way you can act on what is true? |
| • 2. How is it impacting your life: feelings, thoughts, choices? | • 5. If you believed God *knew all things and could do all things*, how would it impact your wants and actions? |
| • 3. What does it show that you believe about God? | • 4. If you believed God was *enough for you*, how would it impact your feelings? |

Chapter 7

# You Are Not Worthless

If I asked you what made you valuable, what would you say? Would you say you are valuable because of what you do or how you look? Are you valuable because of your uniqueness, strengths, and talents? Maybe you're valuable because of what others think of you?

God says you are valuable simply because He made you.

If I handed you a genuine twenty-dollar bill, you would know it was worth twenty dollars, right? However, what if I handed you a piece of paper that I'd drawn on to look sort of like a twenty-dollar bill? You'd know right away that its value wasn't really twenty dollars. Why? Because of who made it.

If I make twenty dollars, it's useless. If the US Mint makes twenty dollars, you can buy twenty dollars' worth of stuff with it. It wouldn't matter if the authentic twenty-dollar bill were super crisp or wrinkled and dirty. It wouldn't matter if someone had folded it into a paper airplane. No matter what, it would be worth twenty dollars solely because of who made it.

The same is true of you. You are not worthless, and nothing you do or don't do can change that. You are immensely valuable because of who made you. When we begin to find our worth and security in God, the One who made us, rather than in what we do, what we look like, or what others think of us, we can flourish.

When we begin to find our worth and security in God, the One who made us, rather than in what we do, what we look like, or what others think of us, we can flourish.

# God Made You Valuable

I homeschool my wonderful kiddos. I'm a teacher at heart, so I love it. I think I end up learning more than they do. This year, we are diving deep into ancient civilizations for history. I enjoyed our unit on the pharaohs and ancient Egypt.

Did you know that, because of its location, King Tut's tomb wasn't discovered until 1922? It had been buried for three thousand years! Since the initial discovery, five thousand artifacts have been uncovered, valued at over $680 million. That's a lot of stuff to bury with a dead guy. And yet, that boy was worth way more than that in God's eyes.

You are worth more than that too. You are of far greater value than $680 million. People have exorbitant value because of who made them.

Austin and I have a friend we met in Durango who now does college ministry with his wife in Texas. Eli and Mandy both love the Lord and want their lives to please Him. God has gifted Eli with stellar musical abilities and the gift to passionately teach God's Word. Every time Eli has a conversation, he wants to share something the Lord taught him.

We once invited Eli to come to Denver to put on a concert and speak to our students. The week he came, we were dealing with a gossip problem with some of them. God orchestrated things so beautifully to have Eli come at that exact moment. He is possibly one of the most honoring people I know. It seems he uses every opportunity to honor people and brag about them. He spoke to our leadership students about honor and taught them what it was and why it's such a big deal, the whole time bragging on Austin and me to the students. The next day, I overheard some of the girls who were involved in the gossip problem—only this time, they were bragging on other people!

When Eli lived in Durango, God challenged him to be a man of honor and not speak against his brothers and sisters in Christ, especially his leaders. Rather, he should be a warrior who defends them. Isn't it interesting that it is most common to talk bad about our spiritual authorities, when they are the exact ones God calls us to honor?

Once during this time, Eli overheard a friend speaking ill about the leader of the ministry, and Eli was so upset that he actually punched the guy. I'm not saying we should go around punching people, but the gossip stopped, and that group of guys started thinking more highly of their leaders. Not long after that, the ministry qua-drupled in size (not that size is necessarily an indication of God's blessing). Honoring others has incredibly rewarding fruit, whereas gossip has incredibly destructive fruit.

Miriam is an example of how seriously God takes dishonor. In Numbers 12, Miriam and Aaron began to talk against their brother Moses because of his foreign (Cushite) wife. Miriam and Aaron were justified in saying he shouldn't have married this woman. But rather than talking to God and Moses about it, they gossiped to each other, and God was not happy about it.

The Lord called them together and addressed Miriam and Aaron's sin in a crazy way. He bragged about Moses! God, creator of the universe, sustainer of all things, the beginning and the end—this God bragged about a human (see vv. 4–8). The One who spoke the Milky Way, the octopus, and cherry trees into being and breathed life into the first man—*He* bragged about Moses. Surely if God, the Perfect One, can consider a person worth bragging about, so can we! Moses deserved respect not because he was so great but because of who made him.

Likewise, Jesus was constantly bragging on people, especially about their faith: the widow who donated her little bit of money, the centurion who knew Jesus could just speak and his servant would be healed, and more (see Mark 12:41–44; Matt. 8:5–10). If Jesus bragged on people, shouldn't we?

I once saw a video taken in Africa on a safari. The video is called *Battle at Kruger*, if you want to look it up on YouTube.[1] Basically, some people filmed lions getting ready to attack a herd of water buffalo. The lions pounce, and the chase is on. One baby water buffalo falls to the back, and the lions grab it. It's super sad, as you think the calf must be dead because many lions surround it. This group is close to the edge of a river or pond, and the next thing you know, a crocodile lurches up, grabs the baby water buffalo, and starts playing tug-of-war with the lions.

The lions win and apparently think they are victorious, when the entire herd of buffalo comes back and surrounds them. Finally, a couple of the bigger buffalo charge the lions and begin to push them around. The lions eventually get scared off. Still, you're left thinking there's no way the calf can be okay. But sure enough, up it pops, and buffalo surround it as others continue to chase the frightened cats away.

It is amazing. When the video is done, you're left in awe at how brave those buffalo were and how they all came to the calf's defense.

This crazy scene in creation gives us a very clear picture of what believers in Christ need to be like. What a picture of how we've got to fight for each other! The Enemy wants to single us out, isolate us, and devour us—and not only us but our brothers and sisters in Christ too. He wants to keep us and them from being effective and contributing the unique giftings we have toward fulfilling the Great Commission for God's glory.

Just like the herd, we have to be willing to get out of our comfort zones and step into dangerous places to protect others, because they are made by God. They are valuable and worthy of being treated with dignity because of who made them. God makes valuable things, and His stuff deserves to be treated as such.

The world will know that God sent Jesus by our love for one another (see John 13:35). That is flat-out mind-blowing and convicting. By our love, our unselfish choosing to work for another's highest good, a nonbelieving world will know that Jesus is Lord. We need to stand with each other and fight for each other even if we disagree on nonessential issues. Jesus' command calls us to believe the best about others and see them through the righteousness of Christ, the way the Lord sees us. We need to fight for and honor each other—not because others deserve it but because it's what the Lord does for us. We need to love because God loved us first.

Just recently, my friend Nicole bragged on Facebook about a local Starbucks employee. She said that whenever she goes there, Marty the Starbucks guy is always so

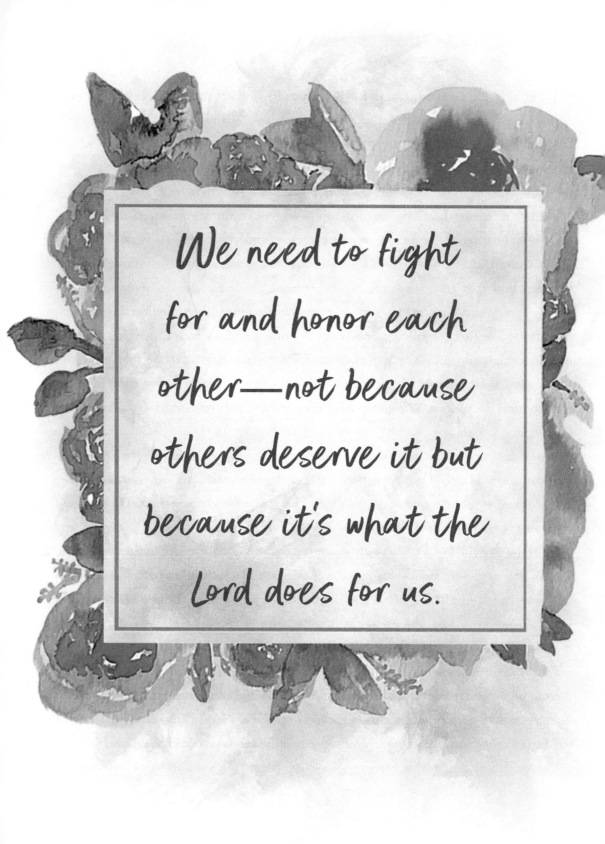

We need to fight for and honor each other—not because others deserve it but because it's what the Lord does for us.

happy as he greets people. One day, she asked his secret. Want to know what he said? "My faith in God. I believe every person I meet is made in His image. So you know, if you really believe that, you treat people a little differently." Wow, right? And then, as she was bragging about Marty on Facebook, other people were chiming in with comments, saying they knew the guy she was talking about because he treats them great too.

Remember our friend Eli and how his ministry grew so much when people were honoring and bragging on each other? I've also seen the opposite happen. I've seen a thriving ministry with 150 students at a tiny hyper-secular college break into pieces, all because of gossip. The students talking about the leaders got completely out of hand, and Satan had a heyday. Within a matter of months, the ministry had only around 30 kids.

People are made in the very image of God and are immensely valuable. They are worthy of being treated with dignity and respect, not because they earned it or deserve it but because of who made them.

## God Can Use You

Since junior high, I've had a desire to disciple other girls. My first years of high school were wasted on my own frivolousness, focused on myself. But in the summer between my sophomore and junior years, a friend invited me to a church camp. I had told her no so many times previously that I felt bad saying no again, and I really didn't have an excuse. So I went.

While I was at this Christian camp, I had an experience with God that changed the trajectory of my life. The worship leader was singing "You Are My All in All." I was moved to raise my arms in surrender to the Lord. I gave Him control of my life, which I had been living for my own pleasure rather than His.

With my arms up and eyes closed, a vivid picture appeared in my mind of a crowd of people, and then Jesus started walking by. I just watched as He was touching people, and when He was almost past me, I shouted, "I love You, Jesus!" He stopped and looked right at me in the large crowd and said, "I love you, Laura." I melted into a thousand pieces. I was struck by the fact that He knew my name.

That night on my bed, I confessed how I had been living as though life was all about me and my fear that I was addicted to drugs and the choices I had made with guys, but I said I wanted Him instead. I told Him I wanted my life to be all about Him. That night, I turned away from my old life, and new desires were birthed in me.

After that summer, I really wanted to disciple girls. I had no idea what that involved, but I knew I wanted to influence them the way God had influenced me. During that time, a particular person didn't take me up on my offer to work with younger girls, and I interpreted that to mean God couldn't use me.

So when I went to college and heard about a ministry called Young Life that would let me disciple girls, I was all in. They trained me in how to go into high schools and meet girls, build relationships with them, and invite them to club and camp. So I did. I went to a basketball game, where I sat myself right down next to Candace, a cute little blonde freshman. We got to talking, and she introduced me to her group of friends. I invited them to lunch, and our friendship was born.

I took those twelve girls to McDonald's each week. They started coming to club, and then they went to camp in the summer, where God brought them each into a relationship with Him. This led to teaching my very first Bible study. I loved these girls and got to see God changing their lives in amazing ways. Years later, one of them even ended up becoming the area director for Young Life. God used a college girl with zero experience to alter the landscape of eternity. And all I did was go to a basketball game and say hi to someone. Long-lasting ripples start with small pebbles.

How inspiring are the stories of people who walked by faith even when they couldn't see the fruit. Hebrews 11 showcases some of these people in a list we call the Hall of Faith. And yet, many more could be added to that list.

Robert Jermain Thomas was one of these people. In 1863, he moved to Shanghai, China, with his new bride so they could be missionaries. Robert was gifted in learning languages and enthusiastic in wanting to talk about Jesus, though his supervisor wanted him to start a school where there would be no talking about the Lord. Robert's wife soon became pregnant, but the conditions in Shanghai were rather dirty, and he didn't feel they were suitable for his baby. So he left for two weeks to search for a different city that would have better living conditions. While he was gone, his wife miscarried their baby and died. The death of his wife and baby, as well as his supervisor's demands, led him to quit.

He found a job working for Customs, where two men from the region that is now North Korea told him about how their government would not allow Bibles or let people hear the gospel. So Robert went to the central part of the Korean peninsula with a bunch of Bibles and began to tell people about Jesus. Though the officials were hostile toward foreigners, he would convince them to each take a gift of a book. When he ran out of Bibles, he went to China to get more.

On his return trip, Korean soldiers were ordered to destroy the ship. They set it on fire, and most of the twenty-two crew members burned to death or drowned. Some passengers reached the shore but were killed by the soldiers. Robert was one of them. As he was about to be killed, he yelled out the name of Jesus in Korean and handed his executioner a Bible. Then he was shot.

The Korean authorities did what they could to reclaim and burn the Bibles that Robert had distributed the length of the Taedong River. However, some of those who had received the Bibles not only held on to them but also read them.

Some who witnessed Robert being shot were greatly impacted and became Christians. Others furthered the gospel unintentionally. One government official named Pak Yong-Sik took home some of the Bibles thrown onto the riverbank and used the pages to wallpaper rooms in his house to display them as trophies of triumph over Christians.

But Robert's impact didn't end there. Around thirty years later, in the early 1890s, Samuel Moffett went to Korea to start churches. He encountered some of the believers who had been influenced by the last mission of Robert Jermain Thomas. He even met the man who had bought the former home of government official Pak Yong-Sik. The walls were still papered with pages from Robert's Bibles. Moffett was able to read them for himself, and he went on to share the gospel with people. The result was a small church established in that very home, which became the first church in that part of Pyongyang, which is now the capital of North Korea.

Fifteen years later, Pyongyang had become a strong Christian center with a hundred churches. This influenced what became South Korea as well. Robert Jermain Thomas took those Bibles to Korea around 160 years ago, and now South Korea is among the most Christianized countries in the world. One man believed God, and a nation was changed.

Another modern-day "hall of faither" was Henrietta Mears. She lived some forty years after Robert Jermain Thomas. She simply started teaching Sunday school. But as God would have it, the class grew and grew. Henrietta lived to make much of Jesus, and she was described as someone who consistently told others about Him.

One time, she shared the gospel at a college meeting where a particular young man was in attendance. His name was Bill Bright. She invited him and others to be part of a six o'clock Saturday morning prayer and Bible study group. Bill ended up putting his faith in Christ, and then he went on to start Campus Crusade for Christ. He described Henrietta as "a master at motivating and inspiring people to do great things for God." He said she taught people about evangelism and discipleship by modeling it right in front of them.[2]

Henrietta influenced many people to live intentionally for the glory of God. At the time of her death, more than four hundred people had gone into Christian service as a result of her influence. The lives she touched included international evangelist Billy Graham, Young Life founder Jim Rayburn, Navigators founder Dawson Trotman, and US Senate Chaplain Richard Halverson. God does the impossible through people who cling to what is true about Him and surrender their lives for His sake.

Neither Robert nor Henrietta ever saw the full impact of their service, and yet their influence continues to ripple in eternity. They invested their lives in God's kingdom rather than their own, and God used them to affect eternity. We will not see the full impact of our own sacrifices till heaven, but it will be worth it.

God is much better at using us to impact eternity than we give Him credit for. He can use us whether we like it or not—and whether we say things perfectly or not. God is bigger than our flaws and weaknesses. After all, if He can use hard-hearted Pharaoh to change the world, surely He can use someone surrendered to Him.

# God Gave You a Purpose

In Genesis, Jesus and two angels appear to Abraham in the form of travelers. Abraham, already ninety-nine years old, *runs* to serve them. During their conversation, he finds out that the Lord is going to destroy Sodom, the city where his nephew, Lot, and Lot's family live.

Abraham pleads with the Lord not to destroy Sodom, and the Lord agrees to withhold destruction if ten righteous people can be found in the city (see Gen. 18:22–33). Unfortunately, there are not even ten, so the city's destruction is sealed. The two angels go to rescue Lot and his family before the city is burned.

When the angels arrive at the gates, Lot insists they stay with him for the night, knowing how vile the city is. That night, men from every part of the city surround Lot's house, yelling for him to send the visitors out so they could rape them. Ugh. Lot goes out to the men and pleads, "No, my friends. Don't do this wicked thing. Look, I have two daughters who have never slept with a man. Let me bring them out to you, and you can do what you like with them. But don't do anything to these men" (19:7–8). Oh my word, what a creep!

The angels pull him back inside the house and strike all the men with blindness so they can't figure out how to get in. Smart move. The angels then explain that the Lord

God is much better
at using us to impact
eternity than we give
Him credit for.

is about to burn down the city, so Lot and his wife and daughters have to get out. But Lot hesitates, and the angels physically yank him, his wife, and their daughters by the hand. They lead the family out of the city, urging, "Flee for your lives! Don't look back, and don't stop anywhere in the plain!" (vv. 16–17).

The Lord rains down burning sulfur on Sodom and Gomorrah, destroying all those in the cities. But Lot's wife looks back, and she is supernaturally transformed into a pillar of salt (see v. 26).

She looked back. It just goes to show how spiritual decline happens both slowly and drastically. We are all capable of looking back, of moving so far from God that we end up longing for things that in any other state of mind we would recognize as horrid. We are each capable of spiritual blindness and of having a deceitful heart that longs for evil. How desperate we are for the Lord's strength and help in aligning our hearts and desires with His.

It comes down to a heart willing to yield. We must surrender to the Lord and let Him fill us with His Spirit. This is how we can find the life that He wants to live through us. Our hearts can easily long for things besides the purposes the Lord has for us. We need to yank ourselves away and start walking toward what He wants.

So what is our purpose? Is it taking care of kids or aging parents? Making a lot of money? Being famous or influential? To make a mark, find a unique voice, live out a destiny, or leave a legacy?

God tells us that our purpose is to glorify Him (see Isa. 43:7; 1 Cor. 10:31).

The Lord wants to make His invisible qualities visible to a lost and dying world, and you in all your uniqueness can do that in a way no one else can. The way you were put together is unlike how any other person alive today or ever in history has been put together. This is how you can be a living example of a little piece of what God is like. You are made in the image of God!

Your life is incredibly valuable because it gives people a glimpse of the God who created them and passionately loves them. Your unique fingerprint and heartbeat are unmatched by even one other person who has ever lived or ever will live. The way God put your body and personality together shows what God is like in a way that only you can demonstrate. And without you, the world would not get to see a very specific truth about God.

Austin and I led a mission trip to Russia in 2008. Russia is a place of unexpected opposites. It is gray and drab, and yet out of nowhere will appear the most beautiful church you have ever seen. Maybe you've seen that candy-looking church in pictures: Saint Basil's Cathedral in Moscow. Most of the other structures around the country are made of bland concrete. So why the color and the beauty in the churches? It's because the builders believed God is beautiful and they wanted to reflect that.

What a perfect illustration of what it means to glorify God. God uses the work of long-dead Russian architects to glorify Himself.

God, the One who built not only our cells but also our souls, says in Isaiah 43:7 that we are created for His glory. How incredible! We don't have to wonder why we exist or what our purpose is in life—the creator and sustainer of life spelled it out for us: our purpose is to glorify God.

Imagine that you and I were sitting at a coffee shop together and you asked, "What is my purpose?" Imagine God materializing at the table, writing something on a piece of paper, and sliding it over to you. You flip it over and read His answer: "Your purpose is to glorify Me." But instead of a little piece of scratch paper, He had Isaiah write out an entire book for you.

God has told you that He created you with a purpose, and it's a very fulfilling purpose: to glorify Him. So this life we've been given is wasted unless we live for the glory of God.

But what does *glorify* mean? Does it mean to sing or praise Him with our words? I believe *glorify* means to behold and reflect, to look at something and display it to others. So to glorify God means to fix your eyes on Him and show the world what He is like; to know God and make Him known.

I love how John Piper explains it in *Don't Waste Your Life*:

Your purpose is to make the invisible God visible to a people desperately loved by their Creator.

God created me—and you—to live with a single, all-embracing, all-transforming passion—namely, a passion to glorify God by enjoying and displaying his supreme excellence in all the spheres of life.[3]

We are put here on earth during this specific time period to see and display God's character. God tells us that as we truly know Him, we will reflect Him: "And we all, who with unveiled faces contemplate the Lord's glory, are being transformed into his image with ever-increasing glory, which comes from the Lord, who is the Spirit" (2 Cor. 3:18). When we see Him as He truly is, we are changed from the inside out by the work of the Holy Spirit, and we begin to reflect Him more and more. We come to resemble what we are gazing at.

So what is your purpose in life? You exist to show a lost and dying world what God is like. Your purpose is to make the invisible God visible to a people desperately loved by their Creator.

But not only were you given the incredible *purpose* of showing people what God is like, you were also given a *mission*. A co-mission with Jesus, you could say. You have been given the great task of making disciples.

Every person has the same purpose in life, and God has also given every Christian a specific mission called the Great Commission: the mission of making disciples through the process of evangelism and discipleship. All believers have the same purpose and the same mission, and yet we are all created very differently. Purpose answers the question "Why do we exist?" Mission answers the question "What are we here to do?" Though we are similar in those ways, we also are all unique and in different seasons and places in life, so how we accomplish our purpose and mission will look very different. Our uniqueness is summed up by the characteristics, gifts, and experiences given to us by God.

I developed a helpful little tool that illustrates this. "Life Direction Circles" is a Venn diagram of three circles. One circle is our mission, one circle is our current reality, and one circle is our uniqueness. Our tendency is to focus on one circle at a time.

Trying to live out our strengths without regard to the other two realms, for example, or wanting to enjoy our current season of life without addressing the other two areas. But living for just one of these circles leads to frustration and ineffectiveness in our callings.

## Living on Purpose for the Glory of God

### Life Direction Circles

Purpose: Answers "Why do we exist?"
Mission: Answers "What are we here to do?"
Uniqueness: INVEST Acronym
Vision: Picture of the desired future. A mental image of
a possible and desirable future state.

*Purpose: To glorify God.*
*To know God and make Him known.*

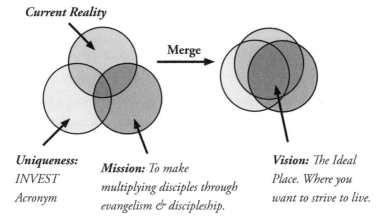

*Current Reality*

Merge

*Uniqueness:*
INVEST
Acronym

*Mission: To make*
*multiplying disciples through*
*evangelism & discipleship.*

*Vision: The Ideal*
*Place. Where you*
*want to strive to live.*

The goal is to merge these circles together as much as possible. Let's take Jesus as our example. He used His *uniqueness* of being able to heal (so people would know He was God) to create opportunities to preach the gospel. His *current reality* was that He was traveling around Galilee to preach the gospel. In Mark 1:29–33, we see, by the fact that Scripture mentions people bringing their friends and family to Jesus to heal, that His *uniqueness* of being able to heal was getting more attention.

So in order to live out His uniqueness without neglecting the mission, He changed up His current reality. "Let's go somewhere else to the towns nearby," He said in verse 38 (NASB), "so that I may also preach there; for this is why I came." He didn't let the message of the gospel (His mission circle, so to speak) get pushed aside by His uniqueness circle (of doing good deeds) or by His current reality circle (preaching in Galilee). He made a change that would allow all three circles to merge.

Entropy, the second law of thermodynamics, says that things naturally go from order to disorder. In nature, things tend to fall apart and decay. It's the same with our life priorities. Unless we are intentional about a plan to merge these circles, it won't happen.

In the following pages, I define mission, uniqueness, and current reality to give you a picture of how to merge your circles. Let's start with current reality.

## Your Current Reality Circle

Though we all have the same 168 hours in a week, no two people have the exact same life situation. Your current reality consists of the specific places you spend your time. It is your unique sphere of influence. You may have a job you work, or you may care for kids or aging parents. These are the spaces where God wants you to live out your purpose and mission.

## Your Mission Circle

God has given you a purpose, which is to glorify Him. He's also given you a mission, one that is captured in the Great Commission announced by the risen Jesus in Matthew 28:18–20.

The Lord is at work in the hearts of people around us, but so often our fears keep us from even getting into conversations to find out what He might be doing in them. Bill Bright says, "Success in witnessing is simply taking the initiative to share Christ in the power of the Holy Spirit and leaving the results up to God."[4] And that really is all we can do: God is the One who changes hearts. However, He has called us to be part of the adventure by telling people His story.

For twenty years, I did not share my faith. I would invite my friends to church and youth group, hoping someone else would share the actual gospel with them. Twenty years is a long time to not be obedient to what God calls us to do. And as Romans 1 talks about, when we disobey God, our hearts become hardened. This is what happened to me.

I went to college wanting to be involved in ministry. I liked the idea of girls coming to know Jesus, and I wanted to be one who would help them grow into strong disciples after they had given their lives to Him. But whenever the topic of evangelism would come up, I had a very arrogant attitude. I distorted the verse "Always be prepared to give an answer to everyone who asks you to give the reason for the hope that you have" (1 Pet. 3:15) by making it mean that you shouldn't go to people but you should wait for them to come to you.

As a result, I would get angry at people who were taking the initiative to share the gospel. I honestly thought, *They're just making my job harder, because now the unbeliever is offended and I'll have to befriend her and win her back.* When I think about my attitude, I am embarrassed about my self-centeredness and pride, and I'm sad about all the opportunities wasted. But praise God that He is able to soften even the hardest of hearts.

I hope you're wondering what happened. How did God change my hard heart? Well, God blessed me with Austin. Austin and his friend John were constantly sharing their faith. At first, it bothered me, thinking they were offending people. But rather than seeing people get offended when Austin and John shared the gospel, they were seeing fruit—people surrendering their lives to Christ. I couldn't believe it.

When I looked back on my Christian life, I had to admit that not one person had ever come up and asked me to share the gospel with them. Sure, there were people who had come to Christ because I'd invited them somewhere, but it was not because I took the initiative to start the conversation with them. Who knew?

So one day I said to Austin, "Okay, walk me through what you say to people when you share the gospel." I wanted to test his words to look for something that would offend me if I were not a believer. God used that conversation to change my heart. Austin explained how he used the Four Spiritual Laws developed by Bill Bright. I was amazed that he did this in a conversational way. He was not cramming anything down anyone's throat. It wasn't a canned presentation but a simple dialogue. I thought, *I can do this.*

So I tried it out. It felt totally normal (once I could work up enough guts to even get into a spiritual conversation), and God blessed His message. I had the joy of seeing eternal fruit born for His kingdom as girls surrendered their lives to Christ because of our conversations.

I don't know what your attitude is about sharing your faith, but I am pretty sure you are not as hard-hearted as I was. And even if you are, would you be willing to let God shape your opinion about it today?

I'm not going to go in-depth here on how to share your faith. But my website, MissionalWomen.com, gives you a ton of resources. There's even an online course that teaches you to share the gospel and merge these circles.

The Great Commission God has given us has two parts: evangelism and discipleship. Now that we've covered the basics of evangelism, let's talk about discipleship.

Discipleship is helping someone become stronger in their relationship with God. I like longtime missionary Roger Hershey's definition of a mature disciple: "one who walks by faith, communicates their faith, and multiplies their faith."[5] So the main goal of discipling someone is helping him or her become able to have a strong relationship with God, share the gospel, disciple others, and teach others to do the same. It's coming alongside believers and pointing them to the Lord and encouraging them to take steps of faith. If you want resources to help you with some practical ways to disciple someone, check out MissionalWomen.com.

And let me remind you that God gave you an incredibly satisfying mission of partnering with Him in His passion to seek and save the lost. But we don't do the Great Commission in order to pay Him back or to not disappoint Him. Living the way God desires is not about us doing things for Him. It's all about surrendering and letting Him live His life through us. We are vessels in His hands to do with as He pleases. Your life is not your own—it was bought with the blood of Jesus. It is His. He gave you a partnership of reconciling people to Him, the joy of seeing dead people come to life and join the team of rescuing others.

When we walk with God, doing what He wants us to do, especially in hard things like sharing the gospel, we are storing up bonding moments with God. These adventures with God deepen our relationship with Him and cause us to know Him more. It's like what Paul wrote to Philemon: "I pray that your partnership with us in the faith may be effective in deepening your understanding of every good thing we share for the sake of Christ" (1:6).

When we deeply realize that we won't lose God's love, it motivates us to love Him back and serve Him all the more. Since He is the One who takes our feeble offerings of service and makes them count for eternity, our role is only to walk with God in surrender and leave the results up to Him.

## Your Uniqueness Circle

Your overall purpose is to glorify God, to know God and show the world what He is like. Your mission is to make disciples through the process of evangelism and discipleship. And your current reality consists of the spheres of influence where God has placed you. And there is one last circle in the diagram: your uniqueness.

You are beautifully unique and valuable because of who God made you. You have unique value because you are an eternally precious masterpiece. You are an eternal-God reflector made in His image. Your unique experiences, values, strengths, passions, and so on show the world what God is like in a way that no one else can.

How we need more Christians living out their unique design! Could you imagine if there were architects going to God, saying, "Lord, in Jeremiah 33:3, You tell me to call to You, and You promise to answer and tell me great, unsearchable things I don't know. So what is the best way to design this building?" Imagine not just architects but scientists, astronomers, environmentalists, politicians, caretakers, teachers, musicians, businesspeople, artists, and doctors all calling out to God, "Oh Lord, teach me how and why!" He is the ultimate source of all these things, and He uses these means to reveal Himself.

It seems like we should know our uniquenesses, but how often do we really sit around and write down the ways God fashioned us? I imagine not very often. I suspect a lot of people aren't even really sure what makes them unique. In order to merge the circles, we have to have a clear picture of what each circle looks like for us individually.

So, to help you know your uniquenesses, here is an acronym I came up with and some questions that allow God to lead us in how we are built to display Him. The acronym is INVEST. It stands for Interests, Nature, Vision, Experiences, Spiritual gifts, and Treasure. Take a minute to ask God to bring to mind any sin you need to confess and surrender, and then ask Him to lead you in answering the following questions.

### Interests
- *What* things or activities and *whom* do you enjoy? (This could be a person, a people group, an age group, etc.)
- What do you see going on around you that, every time you think about it, deeply affects you?

### Nature (or Personality)
- What are some of your strengths and weaknesses, mentally, emotionally, and socially?

### Vision

- What is something in the world that you desperately want to be different?
- What are you passionate about? How would others describe you in terms of your passions?
- What is something you would do in your lifetime for the glory of God if you knew you would not fail?

### Experiences

- What are the top events or activities that have shaped who you are today?
- What has happened in your life that has been greatly influential in shaping what you personally value?

### Spiritual Gifts

- What comes naturally for you to do?
- What do you enjoy doing? What things leave you refreshed and encouraged after you do them?
- What have others noticed you are good at?
- If you have taken spiritual gift inventory tests, what did they say your primary spiritual gifts were?
- What are some things you are confident doing because of the ability God has given you?

### Treasure

- What has God entrusted to you? What resources are you a steward of?

## Merging the Circles

Now comes the fun part: merging the circles together.

Looking at the circles of mission, your current reality, and your uniqueness, what would it look like to live more out of the middle, where all the circles overlap?

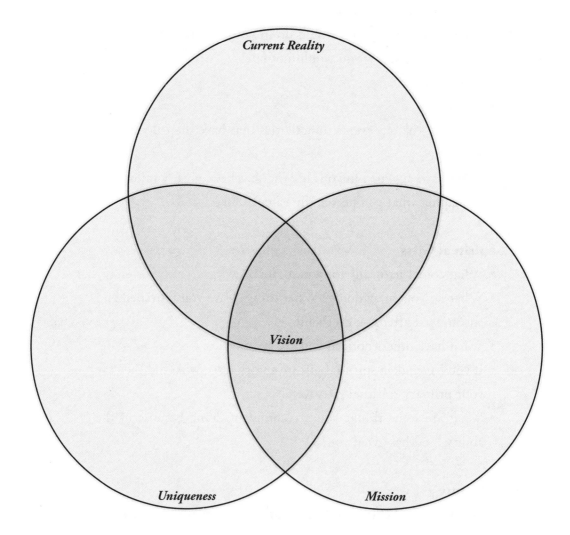

It is such a gift to partner with God to make an eternal impact. The God-given qualities you bring to the table are quite extraordinary. You are valuable, God can use you, and He gave you an eternity-shaping purpose.

What keeps you from feeling like you are valuable?
What keeps you from believing God can use you?
What about your purpose excites you? What about it scares you?

Spend some time talking to God about the things you wrote above.

# CONNECT WITH THE LORD

Watch the chapter 7 video now. Find the video using the QR code or link on page 22.

## God Made You Valuable, Can Use You, and Gave You a Purpose

• Read 2 Samuel 7.

• Write down what you notice about David in the chapter.

• Why does God say no to David building the temple?

• What does this show you about David's purpose and/or mission?

God reminded David of his purpose of glorifying and revealing Him as the Lord Almighty. God had trained David to be a warrior, not an architect. This chapter shows us that not every desire we have that glorifies God is for right now. It might not even be what God has for us to walk in at all. But as we are taking steps of faith, God redirects us. Redirection is not failure. In fact, God even used the redirection in David's life to help him start storing up materials for Solomon to build the temple.

## Truth Chart

| | |
|---|---|
| • 1. In what ways have you felt like you were worthless? | • 6. What is one way you can act on what is true? |
| • 2. How is it impacting your life: feelings, thoughts, choices? | • 5. If you believed God *made you valuable*, how would it impact your wants and actions? |
| • 3. What does it show that you believe about God? | • 4. If you truly believed God *could use you*, how would it impact your feelings? |

# Conclusion

We are created in the image of God for His glory. Who we are is totally wrapped up in what the Craftsman fashioned. From the very fabric of our DNA, God intentionally designed us to reflect a mix of gifts, experiences, and His attributes that not one other person who has ever existed could display.

For example, since the time he could talk, my youngest son, Asa, has shown that he is surprisingly thoughtful. When his sister hit her head, he went to pick her a flower, and when his other sister hurt her knee, he heated up her stuffed-animal heating pad to comfort her. Did I mention the kid is six? Every day I marvel at his ability to think of others.

Someone might think it's because we are such awesome parents, but I beg to differ. I didn't teach him that, and most of my other kids don't have this same level of thoughtfulness. In fact, I haven't even met an adult with the same degree of thoughtfulness. This was put in him by the God who fashioned his cells.

Or take my friend Leah, who has an enthusiasm for life and Jesus that can't be squished even by cancer. Or my friend Linda, who rarely fails to encourage whoever she is talking with, after just a few minutes of conversation. Or my friend Jackie, whose creativity is unmatched. Or my husband, who is a master of details.

God put these qualities in them to show us that *He* is thoughtful, *He* is enthusiastic, *He* is encouraging, *He* is creative, and *He* is detailed. We can marvel at the greatness of God because of how He purposefully designed these people. I get a real, in-my-face, tangible reflection of the character of God by seeing who God made.

God drove this truth home to me not long ago. I am in the same community as a couple of people who have really hurt my family and me. But whenever we see them, I am kind. For a while, I got frustrated with myself about why I was still kind to these people. They didn't deserve it. I wondered if there was something wrong with me. Was I a people-pleaser? Why couldn't I just be neutral or ignore them?

But God stepped into my flawed, lack-of-gospel thinking. First, who was I to say what people deserve? If we got what we deserved, we'd all be in hell. And second, there's nothing wrong with me because I am kind to people who don't deserve it. This behavior reflects the character of God, who gives grace to the ungodly. That characteristic of being kind was put there by God, and I need to make sure I don't squelch it.

I hope the truths that you are not hidden, that you are wanted and not hopeless, that you are not powerless but deeply cared for, that you can't mess up God's plan, and that you have immense value make your faith in the Lord unshakable.

# In Christ I Am ...

Salt and light (Matt. 5:13–14)

Eternally secure (John 10:27–30)

Christ's friend (John 15:15)

Chosen and appointed to bear fruit (John 15:16)

Protected by the power of His name (John 17:11)

Kept from the evil one (John 17:15)

God's gift to Christ (John 17:24)

Justified by faith (Rom. 5:1)

At peace with God (Rom. 5:1)

Rejoicing in trouble (Rom. 5:3)

Reconciled with God (Rom. 5:10)

United with Christ (Rom. 6:5)

Alive (Rom. 6:11)

Freed from the power of sin (Rom. 6:18)

Freed from condemnation (Rom. 8:1)

Indwelt by the Holy Spirit (Rom. 8:9)

A joint heir with Christ (Rom. 8:17)

Having all things work for my good (Rom. 8:28)

Being conformed to the image of Christ (Rom. 8:29)

Inseparable from the love of God (Rom. 8:35)

More than a conqueror (Rom. 8:37)

Accepted (Rom. 15:7)

Given the mind of Christ (1 Cor. 2:16; Phil. 2:5)

Bought with a price (1 Cor. 6:20)

The image of God (1 Cor. 11:7)

A member of the body of Christ (1 Cor. 12:27)

Established, anointed, and sealed (2 Cor. 1:21–22)

Triumphant in Christ (2 Cor. 2:14)

A sweet-smelling aroma manifesting God's presence (2 Cor. 2:14–15)

Adequate (2 Cor. 3:5 NASB)

A new creation (2 Cor. 5:17)

An ambassador for Christ (2 Cor. 5:20)

Righteous (2 Cor. 5:21)

God's coworker (2 Cor. 6:1)

Strong when I am weak (2 Cor. 12:10)

Redeemed (Gal. 3:13)

Liberated (Gal. 5:1)

A saint (Eph. 1:1 HCSB)

Blessed with every spiritual blessing (Eph. 1:3)

Chosen to be holy and blameless (Eph. 1:4)

Adopted (Eph. 1:5)

Enlightened (Eph. 1:18)

Made alive with Christ (Eph. 2:5)

Saved (Eph. 2:8)

A citizen of heaven (Eph. 2:19)

Having the good work begun in me completed (Phil. 1:6)

Being worked in by God (Phil. 2:13)

Rescued from darkness (Col. 1:13)

Experiencing my debt canceled (Col. 1:14; 2:13–14)

Reconciled (Col. 1:21–22)

Presented as holy, faultless, and blameless (Col. 1:22 HCSB)

Rooted in Christ and being built up (Col. 2:7)

Hidden with Christ in God (Col. 3:3)

Being renewed (Col. 3:10)

An expression of the life of Christ (Col. 3:12)

Given a spirit of power, love, and self-discipline (2 Tim. 1:7)

Sanctified (Heb. 2:11)

Holy and given a calling (Heb. 3:1)

Given the right to approach God's throne (Heb. 4:16)

An enemy of the devil (1 Pet. 5:8)

Given exceedingly great and precious promises (2 Pet. 1:4 NKJV)

A child of God (1 John 3:1–2)

Sure to resemble Christ when He returns (1 John 3:2)

Resource 2

# Attributes of God

Advocate (1 John 2:1)

All Sufficient (2 Cor. 9:8)

Almighty (2 Cor. 6:18; Rev. 1:8; 19:15)

Alpha and Omega (Rev. 22:13)

Ancient of Days (Dan. 7:9)

Aseity (Acts 17:25)

Atoning Sacrifice (Rom. 3:25; 1 John 4:10)

Author and Finisher of our faith (Heb. 12:2 NKJV)

Author of Life (Acts 3:15)

Author of Peace (1 Cor. 14:33 NKJV)

Author of Salvation (Heb. 2:10 AMP)

Captain of Salvation (Heb. 2:10 NKJV)

Comforter (John 14:16 AMP)

Consuming Fire (Deut. 4:24)

Cornerstone (Eph. 2:20; 1 Pet. 2:6)

Counselor (Isa. 9:6)

Creator (Isa. 40:28)

Deliverer (Rom. 11:26)

Door (John 10:9 HCSB)

Eternal (Ps. 90:2)

Faithful (Deut. 7:9)

Faithful and True (Rev. 19:11)

Father (1 John 3:1)

Father of Lights (James 1:17)

Father of the fatherless (Ps. 68:5 HCSB)

First and the Last (Isa. 44:6; 48:12)

Good (Ps. 119:68; Rom. 11:22 NKJV)

Gracious (Isa. 30:18; 1 Pet. 2:2–3 NKJV)

Healer (Isa. 53:5)

Help (Ps. 46:1)

High Priest (Heb. 2:17; 3:1)

Holy (Rev. 4:8)

I AM (John 8:58; Ex. 3:14)

Immanuel (Isa. 7:14)

Immeasurable (Ps. 103:11–12)

Immutable (1 Sam. 15:29; James 1:17)

Infinite (Rom. 11:33; 1 Kings 8:27)

Jealous (Ex. 20:5–6)

Judge (James 4:12)

Just (Isa. 26:7; 30:18; Ps. 24:7–10)

Light (1 John 1:5)

Love (1 John 4:8)

Merciful (Deut. 4:31)

Mighty (Deut. 10:17; Isa. 9:6)

Omnipotent (Rev. 19:6)

Omnipresent (Ps. 33:13–14)

Omniscient (Isa. 40:13–14)

Passover Lamb (1 Cor. 5:7)

Providence (Acts 17:25)

Redeemer (Isa. 47:4)

Refuge (Ps. 46:1)

Rewarder (Heb. 11:6)

Righteous (Ps. 145:17)

Rock (Deut. 32:15)

Savior (1 John 4:14)

Shepherd (1 Pet. 5:4; Ps. 23)

Shield (Ps. 84:11)

Sovereign (1 Chron. 29:11–12)

Strength (Ps. 19:14 NKJV)

Trustworthy (Ps. 145:13)

Truth (John 14:6; Titus 1:2)

Victorious (1 Cor. 15:57)

Wisdom (Rom. 11:33)

Wonderful (Isa. 9:6)

Wrath (Ex. 15:7 HCSB; John 3:36)

# Truth Chart Template

Use this template to help you work through your feelings about and reactions to God's work in specific areas of your life.

| | |
|---|---|
| • 1. Feeling: | • 6. What is one way you can act on what is true? |
| • 2. How is it impacting your life in terms of your feelings, thoughts, or choices? | • 5. If you believed number 4 to be *true* about God, how would that influence your feelings and actions? |
| • 3. What does it show that you believe about God? | • 4. What is *true* about God? |

# Notes

## Introduction

1. A. W. Tozer, *The Knowledge of the Holy* (New York: Harper & Row, 1961), 1.

2. Bill Bright, *GOD: Discover His Character*, comp. Nancy Sawyer Schraeder and Helmut Teichert (Orlando: NewLife, 2002), 5.

3. Max Lucado, *It's Not about Me: Rescue from the Life We Thought Would Make Us Happy* (Brentwood, TN: Integrity, 2004), 18–19.

## Chapter 1: You Are Not Hidden

1. See Philippians 2:8; Matthew 27:28; Matthew 26:15; Matthew 1:1; Luke 1:32; Acts 5:31; Luke 19:47; Matthew 20:19; Colossians 1:20; Romans 10:12.

2. See Matthew 27:12; Luke 23:22; John 6:33; John 17:24; John 7:5; Isaiah 9:7; Luke 1:33; Revelation 5:9; Revelation 19:7; 2 Peter 2:9; John 1:10; and Romans 16:25–26.

3. Nick Tate, "Loneliness Rivals Obesity, Smoking as Health Risk," WebMD, May 4, 2018, www.webmd.com/balance/news/20180504/loneliness-rivals-obesity-smoking -as-health-risk.

4. Max Lucado, *It's Not about Me: Rescue from the Life We Thought Would Make Us Happy* (Brentwood, TN: Integrity, 2004), 19.

## Chapter 2: You Are Wanted

1. Definify, s.v. "enjoy," Webster 1913 Edition, accessed July 12, 2022, www.definify .com/word/enjoy.

2. Louie Giglio, *Indescribable: 100 Devotions for Kids about God and Science* (Nashville: Thomas Nelson, 2017), 107.

3. Steve DeWitt, "Loneliness Has Been My Faithful Friend," The Journey, accessed July 6, 2022, www.thejourney.fm/articles/2020/5/18/loneliness-has-been-my-faithful -friend.

4. Warren W. Wiersbe, *The Wiersbe Bible Commentary: New Testament* (Colorado Springs: David C Cook, 2007), 45.

5. Louie Giglio (@louiegiglio), Twitter, January 31, 2014, 11:16 p.m., https://twitter .com/louiegiglio/status/429498570710867968.

## Chapter 3: You Are Not Hopeless

1. Stephanie Fast, *She Is Mine: A War Orphan's Incredible Journey of Survival* (Aloha, OR: Destiny Ministries, 2014).

2. "Boasting," featuring Anthony Evans, on Lecrae, *Rehab*, Reach Records, 2010.

3. Some of this material is drawn from "What should we learn from the story of the rich man and Lazarus in Luke 16?," Got Questions, accessed August 16, 2022, www.gotquestions.org/rich-man-and-Lazarus.html.

4. Scotty Smith, *Objects of His Affection: Coming Alive to the Compelling Love of God* (West Monroe, LA: Howard, 2001), 35–36.

5. "Haven't Seen It Yet," on Danny Gokey, *Haven't Seen It Yet*, Capitol CMG, 2019.

6. Amy and Dave Otteson, *Giving Up Gore: When Our Worst Fear Became Our Greatest Gift*, 2nd ed. (Littleton, CO: Armory, 2017).

## Chapter 4: You Are Not Powerless

1. "Don't Ever Say You're Not Good Enough," Daily Awesome Quotes, March 5, 2013, https://dailyawesomequotes.wordpress.com/2013/03/05/dont-ever-say-youre-not-good-enough.

2. Deirdre E. Donnelly and Patrick J. Morrison, "Hereditary Gigantism—the biblical giant Goliath and his brother," *The Ulster Medical Journal* 83, no. 2 (May 2014): 86–87, www.ncbi.nlm.nih.gov/pmc/articles/PMC4113151.

3. Donnelly and Morrison, "Hereditary Gigantism," 87.

4. Donnelly and Morrison, "Hereditary Gigantism," 87.

5. "David's Sling and Stones—Were they toys or serious weapons?," ChristianAnswers.net, accessed July 21, 2022, https://christiananswers.net/q-abr /abr-slingsforkids.html.

## Chapter 5: You Are Cared For

1. Joanna Klein, "The Gooey Details Behind a Glow Worm's Starry Night Illusions," *New York Times*, December 16, 2016, www.nytimes.com/2016/12/16 /science/glow-worms-new-zealand.html.

2. "Creatures of Light: The Chemistry of Bioluminescence," PBS, accessed July 21, 2022, https://rmpbs.pbslearningmedia.org/resource/nvcol-sci-biolumine/wgbh -nova-creatures-of-light-the-chemistry-of-bioluminescence.

3. As sung by Tauren Wells in "Known," on *Hills and Valleys*, Capitol CMG, 2017.

## Chapter 6: You Can't Mess Up God's Plan

1. From the introduction to the long version of "Now and Forevermore," featuring David Ruis, on *Shake Off the Dust*, Vineyard Music, 2004, www.youtube.com /watch?v=lhLha7XjEmw.

2. Drawn from *The Privileged Planet*, directed by Lad Allen, featuring John Rhys-Davies (La Mirada, CA: Illustra Media, 2010), DVD.

3. Peter W. Stoner and Robert C. Newman, *Science Speaks: Proof of the Accuracy of Prophecy and the Bible*, ed. Don W. Stoner, rev. ed. (Chicago: Moody, 1976; online edition, 2005), chap. 3, www.dstoner.net/Science_Speaks.

4. "Lollipops with Side Effects: A Plant's Sugary Offering Betrays Caterpillars to Predatory Ants," ScienceDaily, April 26, 2011, www.sciencedaily.com/releases /2011/04/110425153558.htm.

5. Farris Jabr, "Calling All Predators: Caterpillar Saliva May Be a Component in Plants' Chemical Alarms," *Scientific American*, August 26, 2010, www.scientificamerican.com/article/caterpillars-betray-location.

6. Smriti Rao, "How the Tobacco Plant Outwitted the Hawkmoth," *Discover*, January 22, 2010, www.discovermagazine.com/environment/how-the-tobacco -plant-outwitted-the-hawkmoth.

7. Bill Bright, *GOD: Discover His Character*, comp. Nancy Sawyer Schraeder and Helmut Teichert (Orlando: NewLife, 2002).

8. "Milky Way," Western Washington University, accessed July 13, 2022, www.wwu.edu/astro101/a101_milkyway.shtml.

9. Fraser Cain, "Are There More Stars or Grains of Sand?," Universe Today, November 25, 2013, www.universetoday.com/106725/are-there-more-grains -of-sand-than-stars.

10. "Strong's H4216—mazzārâ," Blue Letter Bible, accessed August 16, 2022, www.blueletterbible.org/search/search.cfm?Criteria=mazzaroth&t=KJV#s=s_lexiconc.

11. Jason Goodyer, "Cave Paintings Reveal Ancient Europeans' Knowledge of the Stars," Science Focus, January 29, 2019, www.sciencefocus.com/planet-earth /cave-paintings-reveal-ancient-europeans-knowledge-of-the-stars.

12. "5608. saphar," *Strong's Concordance*, Bible Hub, accessed August 16, 2022, https://biblehub.com/hebrew/5608.htm.

13. Ethelbert William Bullinger, *The Witness of the Stars* (London, 1893; Project Gutenberg, 2015), chap. 1, www.gutenberg.org/files/49018/49018-h/49018-h .html#toc7.

14. Barry Setterfield, "Is There a Gospel in the Stars?," Genesis Science Research, accessed July 13, 2022, www.barrysetterfield.org/stargospel.html#virgo.

15. Bullinger, *Witness of the Stars*, chap. 1.

16. Setterfield, "Is There a Gospel."

## Chapter 7: You Are Not Worthless

1. David Budzinski and Jason Schlosberg, "Battle at Kruger," Kruger National Park, South Africa, filmed 2004, YouTube video, www.youtube.com/watch ?v=LU8DDYz68kM.

2. Bill Bright in Judy Douglass, "The Amazing Legacy of Henrietta Mears," Judy Douglass, March 8, 2013, https://judydouglass.com/blog/2013/03/the-amazing -legacy-of-henrietta-mears.

3. John Piper, *Don't Waste Your Life* (Wheaton, IL: Crossway Books, 2003), 31.

4. "Successful Witnessing," Cru, accessed July 7, 2022, www.cru.org/content/dam /cru/legacy/2012/01/successfulwitnessing.pdf.

5. Roger Hershey, in "Compass," Cru, accessed July 7, 2022, www.cru.org/car/en /train-and-grow/bible-studies/compass.html.

# START AN UNSHAKEN GROUP

## WHY?

In today's busy world it's more common than ever to live isolated, lonely, and disconnected but God created us for connection. Join our Unshaken community to connect, pray, and study God's Word with other women who long to stand strong in who they are meant to be.

## WHAT?

A Christian women's small group that meets regularly in person or online with leadership materials created and provided by author and ministry leader, Laura Krokos.

## HOW?

Find the leaders guide and more resources at **MissionalWomen.com**

**MissionalWomen.com** is built to give you resources and help you live on mission for the glory of God.

- Online Courses
- Bible studies
- Ministry tools & Training
- Blog articles
- Video Bible Studies
- Other fun things like digital prints and stickers

Facebook.com/missionalwom
Instagram.com/laurakrokos
YouTube.com/laurakrokos
Pinterest.com/missionalwomen
TikTok.com/@laurakrokos
#youareunshaken to meet others living unshaken lives

MissionalWomen.com

# etherpress

estherpress

*Our journey invites us deeper into God's Word*, where wisdom waits to renew our minds and where the Holy Spirit meets us in discernment that empowers bold action for such a time as this.

*If we have the courage to say yes to our calling and no to everything else, will the world be ready?*

## JOIN US IN COURAGEOUS LIVING

Your Esther Press purchase helps to equip, encourage, and disciple women around the globe with practical assistance and spiritual mentoring to help them become strong leaders and faithful followers of Jesus.

An imprint of

DAVID C COOK

*transforming lives together*